UNFORGETTABLE FACES & STORIES

LETTERS TO HEAVEN

Eileen Doyon

October Hill, LLC

Andrew: Enjoy these amazing letters. You will cry, pass the tissues please! Eileen Doyon 5-20-15

Published by October Hill, LLC

PO Box 693 | Greenland, NH 03840

www.unforgettablefacesandstories.com

Layout and cover design by

Kirsten Larsen Schultz | LarsenEdge Marketing Services

www.larsenedge.com

Back photo courtesy of Fred Wehner

Printed in the United States of America.

ISBN: 0692377840

ISBN-13: 978-0692377840

Thank you for purchasing Letters To Heaven! We are very excited about this fifth book in the Unforgettable Faces & Stories series.

A percentage of profits from Letters To Heaven will go to charity. For each book in the Unforgettable Faces & Stories series we select a charity to send a portion of proceeds from books sales to. It's our way of helping out in our community. Other books / charities in the Unforgettable Faces & Stories series:

Dedications: Dads & Daughters / Wounded Warrior Project

Keepsakes: Treasures from the Heart / Cancer Research

Best Friends: Forever & Ever / Big Brother, Big Sister

Pet Tales: Unconditional Love / NEADS, Dogs for Deaf and Disabled Americans

We'd appreciate your help in getting the word out about us. Here are a few ways you can help:

- ✓ Like / share our Facebook page: www.facebook.com/unforgettablefacesandstories
- ✓ Review our book on Amazon
- ✓ Review our book on Barnes & Noble
- ✓ Send us a video testimonial (You can see sample testimonials on our website: www.unforgettablefacesandstories.com/videos or on our YouTube channel www.youtube.com/user/FacesandStories.

  We love written testimonials too!

Thank you again for your support! We would love for you to participate in one of our upcoming books…YOUR story told by YOU!

THANK YOU

Unforgettable Faces and Stories has a new look! Letters To Heaven is our first self-published book in the series and we are very excited about this! We would like to personally say "Thank You" to all of our contributors since our first book Dedications: Dads & Daughters was published in 2013. We look forward in reading YOUR Story Told by YOU in one of our future books!

INTRO

I lost my dad in 2011 to lung cancer. Being supposedly a grown adult woman I can honestly say that I have never experienced such a deep feeling of loss and felt a piece of my heart torn off. Even after losing my mom and my brother in 1981, this loss was devastating.

Loss adds a new dimension to your life. It changes you. Loss comes in different avenues besides death, there is divorce, loss of a job, loss of a home, even loss of direction in life, but they all have a common thread........they change you.

Through the healing process, we have to deal with all kinds of emotions, feelings, and sufferings to figure it out for ourselves.

Letters To Heaven gives people an opportunity to speak words and ask questions of loved ones who have died. We all have so many unanswered questions still to ask, and stories to tell. Letters To Heaven helps us deal with the pain and healing.

As you read these letters, the words will touch your heart, and make you cry, and you will reflect on people who have died in your own life with unanswered words. We need storytelling to help us make sense and come to peace with the hurting and painful feelings. In this fast world of computers and technology, Unforgettable Faces and Stories gives YOU an opportunity to share YOUR story with others.

So sit back, grab some tissues and open your heart to these amazing men and women as they share with you their own Letters To Heaven to someone very special in their lives.

DEDICATION

We would like to dedicate this book to all of the people that had letters sent to them in this series….Letters To Heaven. You are thought of and remembered each and every day!

AUGUSTUS WHIBLE

BETTY MAY BOBER HANNON

BRENDAN RYAN

BUFORD WAYNE WHITLEY "BITS"

CAPT. FRED H. GODFREY SR.

CARL

HELEN LESZCZYNSKI KITCHNER

CAROLINE BAROT

CASIMIR THADDEUS ZWARYCK

DONALD G. HABERMAN

DORIS ADALAIDE NICHOLS

DUANE TURNER

EDWARD F. BERTOGLIO

ELBERT CALHOUN JR.

FRANCIS X LUCAS

FREDERICK RAYMOND HANCOCK II

GARY MUCHA

GLORIA MARIE CALANDRIELLO PITOCCHELLI

HELEN CREIGHTON

ILA GAUTHIER

JANET FLYNN

JANET LOGAN

JAXSON TURNER

JEANIE COOSE

JIMMIE LEE TRUMAN

LAVERN THOMPSON

LUDWIKA "LUCY" PRENETA DONBECK

MARIE SANTOSUOSSO

MEGAN MILLER

MIKE PELLETIER

RICK JACOBS

ROBERT ALEXANDER

ROBERT DONBECK

ROBERT ETHER

ROBERT TUNNO

ROGER PRATT

RORIE SIMMONS JOSLIN

ROSCOE CASSIDY

SARAH ELIZABETH HOVIS GARRISON

SCOTT MARRACINO

SHARON BENKO

SHIRLEY ANN THOMPSON

TAWNEY STAR SCHMIDT

URSULA PREUSS

VINCENZO "JAMES" ANGELO PITOCCHELLI

Unforgettable faces & stories

Letters to Heaven

Aisling Spofford

BRENDAN RYAN

I am writing this letter for my brother Brendan Ryan. He died on May 20th, 2009. He was 25, I was 19. Brendan had a job that he loved as a quality control technician at Chroma Technology in Vermont. The morning of May 20th, 2009 he and a few of his co-workers were out for a walk behind Chroma when suddenly Brendan collapsed and went into cardiac arrest. Brendan was born deaf and also with Prolonged QT Syndrome. A person that has Prolonged QT Syndrome can suffer from seizures which can also be fatal, causing you to go into cardiac arrest. Our oldest brother, Danny, also died from Prolonged QT Syndrome two years before I was born when he was just about six years old in 1987. Back then they didn't know it was the PQTS since there wasn't that much knowledge about it at the time and assumed the seizures were due to epilepsy. Danny's death revealed what it really was and Brendan was put on medications which helped him live as long as he did.

Dear Brendan,

I've tried writing this letter numerous times before. I could never bring myself to finish it because I still haven't fully accepted the fact that you're gone and I probably never will. There are some days I can't stop thinking about childhood memories that we shared. Like when we played board games, our many adventures during our nature walks in the woods and our day trips up to Schroon Lake with mom and dad. I also constantly remember the last day that I saw you. Mom, Lorelai & I went out to visit you in Vermont. We went out for lunch at a train car restaurant nearby. Lorelai tried to keep a stuffed animal penguin from your collection. We had root beer floats. I'll never forget the root beer floats. Then there are some days when I can't help but sit and cry that I can't see you or talk to you. You're not off to college or living at your new apartment in Vermont anymore.

The day you died was also the same day I found out that I was pregnant with my second daughter, Fiona. I wanted you to be one of the first to know just like when I was pregnant with Lorelai. Lorelai's first birthday was three days away. I was planning her birthday party at Ann & Richard's. You were going to be there for it. You had also planned on helping me pack up everything in my apartment to help me move back into mom & dads. That morning when dad called my cell phone to tell me that he and mom were heading out to Vermont I just assumed that it was just one of their usual visits to see you. Then dad said that you died. That's all that kept echoing in my ears that day. I couldn't let myself believe it. Not until the day I saw you at your wake. The moment I saw you, it was like a flood of sadness and anger inside of me. You were 25 years old with a brilliant mind, a thirst for knowledge and a true love of life.

I couldn't stop asking why. Why couldn't you live a full life into old age like we had always talked about? Why couldn't you make new discoveries like you had always dreamed of? Why couldn't you travel to all the places you wanted to visit? Why couldn't you read all the books you wanted to read? Why couldn't you just live? The fact that you died was too much for me to bear. I pushed it away into the back of my mind and focused on taking care of Lorelai and my pregnancy with Fiona. Ignoring it made me spiral into a depression that took so long for me to recognize and get out of.

Now here I am almost six years later. I'll be 26 this summer. You now have three nieces, Lorelai, Fiona and Keira. Jon and I were married last spring. Jon helped me deal with my grief and made me see everything for the better. All three of your nieces ask about you sometimes and they have picked up some sign language from me as they've grown. I still take a lot of pictures and write like you always encouraged me to do. There have even been a few moments where I've felt like you were right there with me, I swear I could even smell your scent.

You gave me my love of learning, reading, writing, imagination and more. I share those loves with the girls each and every day. Most of the time I remember the good things & feelings. I focus on how proud I was of you graduating salutatorian of your high school class and the amazing speech that you gave. You were and still are an inspiration. I may not have been as book smart as you, which sometimes I was jealous of, but I try to learn new things every day no matter what. You're one of the few people that were always completely honest, true to yourself and always willing to help. You were always there to listen and talk which I miss very much. Being an only child now is a very lonely feeling. Thinking of your smile, your laugh & your bear hugs bring me comfort. I've even had dreams where you've come back home. In some of them you were just lost, in others you could only stay for a day. Maybe one day I will see you again. Until then I will keep picturing you with our other family members that have passed away as well as having many conversations with your biggest heroes such as Carl Sagan and Albert Einstein. As we've said before, we are all stardust. I miss you and love you.

Sincerely,

Forever your little sister, Aisling

Author, Aisling Spofford
http://www.facebook.com
/HarperRayneSeries

Alice Savasta

CAPT. FRED H. GODFREY SR.

Dear Dad,

Remembering you and mother always, and as I go through Fort Edward I am reminded of what a great person you were. You were working on the tugboats on the river and canal and then home to Fort Edward for ten days a month. You loved being home in Fort Edward. You took first aid instructions when you were working the boats. This was because you had a crew working for you and wanted to be able to handle medical emergencies. You just loved first aid and decided to be an instructor taking lessons from the Red Cross whenever you were able to.

You decided Fort Edward needed a rescue squad and an ambulance service and you were going to make sure we had it by doing it yourself. You were great friends with Steve Brown, who had a trucking business on Burgoyne Ave. Steve Brown and David Viele were your first students, and also your oldest two sons, Larry and Fred Jr. They helped form the first rescue squad. Fred Jr. was with the squad til he died but Larry had a hard time with some of his first patients which were children in a bad accident. Larry helped, but he had such a hard time getting sick himself around hurt children plus starting his own family, he left the squad.

Your little classes turned into big groups and the Fort Edward Rescue Squad was formed. The phone line to the squad was my mother's kitchen. She would have to call men at their homes or where they worked when she had a call for them to go out on.

The Rescue Squad was still operating out of Steve Brown's garage but they were working on getting their own place. To receive money from the state, they had to have their own investments. My father put up two houses for the mortgage which was fine with my mother.

The first ambulance was a used one. Floyd Mayrand, Marge Mayrand, and my mother and father drove to Buffalo, New York to buy it and drive it back.

The Rescue Squad grew and you kept teaching first aid along with others. Before long Fort Edward was completely covered. Then you went to South Glens Falls and helped them start a Rescue Squad.

I wish you could see it today. A really beautiful building on Schyular Street on the lot you picked out. We have well trained men with twenty four hour coverage.

You did a beautiful job and instead of resting, you decided Fort Edward needed a nursing home for the sick elderly. Another mortgage on Mother's houses, but the Fort Hudson Nursing Home came into being, and was a beautiful thing for Fort Edward. You had a beautiful dream and you got it. The day the Fort Hudson opened, a beautiful piece was featured in the Post Star Newspaper about your story of the nursing home and how you got it to come about. The family will always love you and are always so proud.

Love, Alice

APRIL MCGINNIS

SHIRLEY ANN THOMPSON

This letter is to my mother, Shirley Ann Thompson who passed away on January 7th, 2011 at that age of 66. She had been diagnosed with Leukemia. I was 43 years old.

Dear Mom,

I spent years confused and angry, always blaming myself for something that would have caused you to leave. I was a well enough behaved little girl, so why wouldn't you love me enough to want to be my mother and raise me and help me become a successful human being. For several years you sent pictures of yourself and letters and on occasion, cards with money; none of this answered any of my questions, instead it left me even more confused and curious. I saw you twice between the ages of 10 and 14, those were sweet times for me but I was becoming a different sort of person that had grown accustomed to not having a mom. When Sis moved us back to Indiana, you got in touch with me. I spent all of those weekends with you but somehow it seemed I was the parent, the one taking care of you. I eventually moved away and it took years for me to allow you in my life again.

When I was a child you leaving me and Teresa was abandonment of the most heartbreaking kind. To basically reject your children, beautiful, talented and witty, tow- headed girls at that, was unfathomable for me. I realize now as an adult, that you were battling demons. I could not understand, that your chaotic life, no matter how exposed to me, was not something I could begin to comprehend. I recognize now that you were an alcoholic, an addict and that you struggled emotionally, so to take care of children alone with no support from anyone, was a task that you simply were not equipped to handle. As a child, I knew that you were prone to days of emotional detachment, depression and resentment and that we were mostly on our own. You taught us early to take care of ourselves, and to take up for each other. I was the baby and you always referred to me as the baby, in fact, I recall that we were once in a minor car accident and you were yelling "is the baby ok", the person who came to our rescue was literally searching for a baby. I was about 5 years old at the time but I would forever be your baby, April Michelle.

At 22 I got married and moved to North Carolina and quickly started a family. I sent you pictures and letters, I even brought Chelsea Ann to meet you when she was 6 months old but I had made up my mind that I would not permit you to be in our lives and that was totally out of fear of what you would do to me emotionally; I was fearful that somehow you would reject my family. I did not have an open heart at that point when it came to having a relationship with you or allowing you to be a Grandmother to my babies. I was still very dejected and hurt with the past that we shared.

After I moved back to Indiana, my life as I knew it began to change. I finally decided to force myself to get to know you, to be determined to find the real you in the hard exterior of a woman who had not brought much to my life, except a lot of frustration and pain. I never once imagined that I would find such an amazingly compassionate, intelligent and comedic person. Mom, the memories I have of you and me at your kitchen table, us both drinking endless cups of coffee, you smoking incessantly and me needing my inhaler, laughing until we were crying, those memories can carry me through some very painful and empty days. You made such an impact on me those last several years but mainly the months between your diagnoses and your passing; those months changed my life forever, those months taught me that taking people for granted is simply a shame, a crime of sorts, one to be forever regretted and never repeated.

The personal outcome from a childhood without you providing me the nurturing love and guidance that I required has not had the negative impact it could have had. I fiercely love my children and will protect them until my last breath. My adult life has mostly been dedicated to making certain that my children know that they are loved and cherished no matter what life brings them, no matter what I am personally experiencing. I am sorry that I did not allow them the opportunity to meet you until the end; I am convinced that they would have appreciated you for the woman you were striving to be and that if given more time, you would have made wonderful memories with them as well. They were such troopers Mom, when you passed, especially Chelsea Ann. She was strong for you and me the day I had to make arrangements. I am a strong and determined woman because of what I experienced in my life, beginning as a child needing her mother, no matter how unhealthy it was at the time, that strength has allowed me to raise children who can be strong in the wake of adversity and chaos. I learned from your mistakes and shortcomings, as I know my children will learn from mine. I learned from you, that we don't always know the core of a person until we have allowed our minds and hearts to really be open for the possibility of who they may be. I discovered in you, to accept where I am but to try to move forward. You taught me resolve and resourcefulness, you taught me to lace up my sneakers and walk my path the best that I can no matter what seems to be following me. You taught me that hard work is necessary and that if any bill gets paid, it should always be the mortgage payment. Most importantly you taught me to walk a path of kindness and leave no one behind. You taught me to reach out in love and acceptance and to touch as many people as possible in a positive way.

The day we were told you had Leukemia, I remember thinking this is it, this is how it all ends. My mother who I have just honestly found is now going to be torn from me again with more pain and devastation than the first time. It has been almost four years since you went to be with your angels but I still reach for the phone to call you in good times and bad. I miss you every single day and I see you in so many things. I hear your voice in my own and I am reminded of you when I laugh with Teresa. We miss you so much and our hearts are still broken in little pieces but we are grateful for your sense of humor and your infectious laugh that we are so blessed to have inherited. Those last memories of you will always be cherished.

I will always love you with all of the pieces of my heart,

April Michelle

"But there's a story behind everything. How a picture got on a wall. How a scar got on your face. Sometimes the stories are simple, and sometimes they are hard and heartbreaking. But behind all your stories is always your mother's story, because hers is where yours begin."

- Mitch Albom

ASHLYNN MARRACINO

SCOTT MARRACINO

Died at 31; I was 11 when he passed of a brain aneurysm.

Dear Dad

You have missed so much, and I feel like I finally understand everything. When I saw you in the hospital and mom said I could talk to you, I was scared, I have never seen anyone in that way. You had tubes and just lying there. So peaceful and quiet, I mean I know it was you, but you looked so different. I was used to seeing you up and talking and laughing. I kept thinking you would just wake up, well, I hoped and prayed. I wish I had talked to you! I never really believed you were with me, but now, I know you are. Before all this, I started to lose confidence in myself and in my faith that you were still with me. I was not seeing the signs and I felt really sad and alone. I definitely now feel a difference in my heart and I have a confidence that you are guiding me through my life. I'm a junior now and my hopes of going to Humboldt are getting closer! I have continued to play softball and other sports. I don't know if you know this, but in 7th grade, I got athlete of the year for all girls of the whole school. Everyone was so surprised, and so was I! I met a guy, and I remember you said I can't date till I was 35, sorry, but he is a great guy. You would like him, he is smart and funny and he makes me laugh. You've always wanted the best for me and you did it! Did you get the other balloons I sent? I know I missed one year but I hope you saw the others. This last one you guided really far, I don't know how but somehow you did it! You helped that balloon travel 436 miles to the right person! She is such a sweet woman who started something we like to call "pay it forward" its when you do something nice for one person and that person will do something nice for another, and another and hopefully it will travel to all people and come back to you. I've inspired so many people and helped people with their loss through a Facebook page, but they honestly have helped me. It feels amazing to be able to help people out just like how you wanted to help people. Also my coach and people all round Whittier are going to help me so I can play travel ball again! So I can be scouted by the Humboldt coach and my dreams of playing college softball will come true! Also people at Humboldt are starting a page where people can donate money so I can attend college! Everyone who has been supportive and helping me are so amazing and I know you would be proud of me and just want the best for me dad. I know your looking down smiling at me because this was your plan the whole time. Even though I can't hug you, and tell you thanks personally, one day, I know we will be reunited again and I can give you the biggest hug ever! By the way, I still have all the letters and drawings you sent to me. I hope you know that the times I get mad, I'm not mad at you, I just want you here with me. I hope you will continue to help me get those homeruns! I love you dad!

Always,

Your little angel, Ashlynn

Facebook page "Letter's to Heaven"

Email: letterstoheaven05@yahoo.com

CAROLYN TURNER

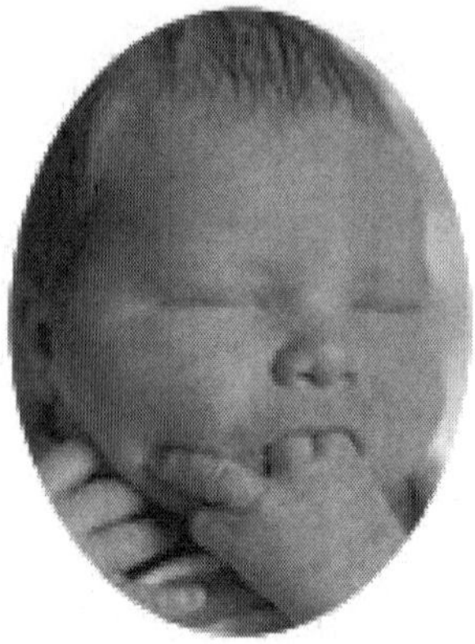

JAXSON TURNER

Dear Jaxson,

How is Heaven? We miss you down here...oh so much. You are considered a hero because you saved lives with organ donation, including a baby girl with your heart. Her name is Allie. You were only 8 weeks old when you left this world in December 2013. Everyone misses you so much...mommy, daddy, your big brother James, your big sisters, Alina, and Laylah-Grace. Now you have a baby sister to watch over as well, her name is Jordyn-Ann.

James misses you so much, he cries for you almost daily as do mommy and daddy. It makes us sad. Allie is doing great with your heart and we know you watch over her and her family daily. Your heart is so perfect for her. Jaxson, we will never forget you, even though you were only with us a short time..you impacted a lot of lives in your short life. I wonder every day who you would be today. Would you have loved wrestling and football like daddy or like singing like mommy? Please send me signs to let me know you are still watching over us. We would have loved to see you grow up and see the boy and man you would have become.

Love, Mommy, daddy, James, Alina, Laylah-Grace, and Jordyn-Ann.

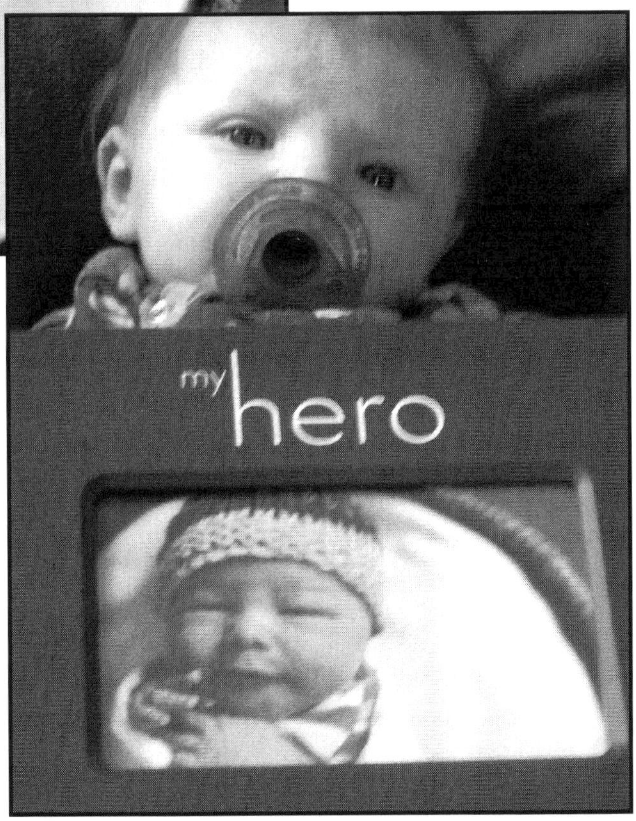
my hero

DIANNE HOLLAND

BETTY MAY BOBER HANNON

Hi Mom, Just wanted to let you know I miss you and think of you all the time. Have you seen dad up there in Heaven? Knowing him, he is probably painting a house or store somewhere, if not, he is playing golf. When you see him, tell him I love him and miss him too. I look out the kitchen window while doing dishes and expect to see him in his truck in our driveway. The mobile home he had is gone now. That is another thing I miss. Dad and I had some good times there. We had a family reunion a year before he passed. Dad, Donald, and Uncle Frankie showed up. What a surprise! I didn't think they would make it. If you see them, please give them my love. I miss them too. I only have one uncle left. They have all left except Uncle Frankie. He is 86 now and is staying with Cathy and Dave.

Have I told you I miss and love you lately? Well just a little about what is going on in my life (like you don't know) I beat breast cancer for now. Still not up to where I would like to be. I miss not having you here when I was going thru it all. It would have been wonderful to have had you wiping my forehead like you did so many times when I would get sick as a child, teenager, and young woman. If I could have had children, I would have been just like you, gentle, kind, and happy. I remember the stories you told me about things that happened when you were young. You and your brothers….oh boy! What stories they were. Did you really like the hair cut grandpa gave you because you laughed at the boy's hair? What ever happened to the boots Uncle Joe took off the steps of the house then when he was home, he cut a piece of wooden block to fill up the heel so you could wear them to go to school and back because you didn't have shoes. He was a good brother and the oldest, so I guess he took care of all of you.

When you got sick and hospice came into the hospital, I told them I would take care of you there. That night, the nurse pushed the empty bed up next to you so I could stay with you. I held your hand and we fell asleep. The problem was that I woke up and you didn't. There were so many things I wanted to ask you and things I wanted to tell you. Now I think you will read my mind and know everything I do, say, and feel. I know you are in the Lord's world and happy. I'm here in a very sad place missing all of you very much. I have friends that are very good to me and we do lots of things like I help pass out food for the needy at church. I like doing things that keep me going and busy just like you did. You were always busy. I'm not that busy yet, but I want to be just like you were.

I know you probably know all of what I said, but you will read my Letter and I know you will be happy about it all. I'm so glad that God put me in your hands to love and raise.

You are the best mother I could have had. We will be together again. Bye for now.

Your loving daughter,

Diane

Diane Crystal Hannon Holland

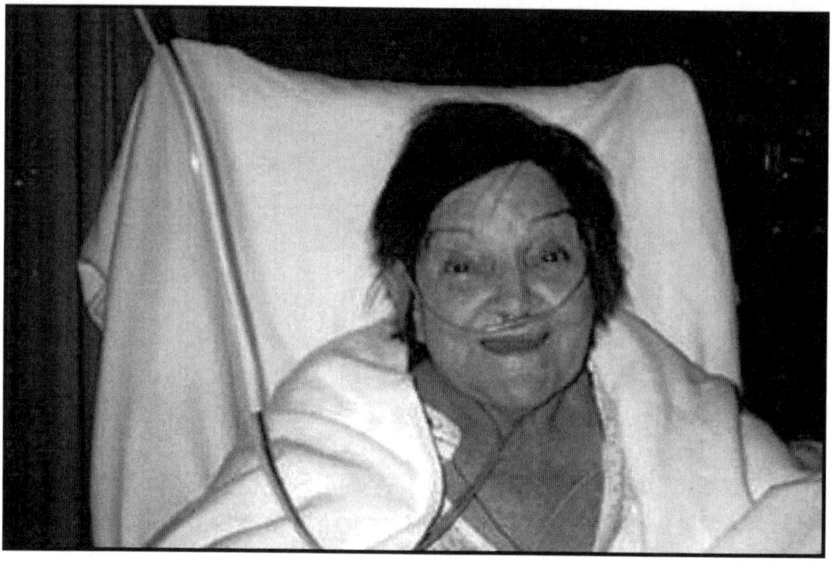

ED BREWSTER

AUGUSTUS WHIBLE

Died in 1999 at the age of 97 of natural causes; I was 37. Thank You DAD

Dear Dad,

Hi, it's been a while, sorry about that. I'm writing this for a lot of reasons. First and foremost to say thank you. (You will see why) Right now, you're throwing me my gloves, telling me to shut up and gas up the saws, but as usual I ignore you and continue talking. (Ignoring you was what I did alone with you, never in front of mom) I never did ignore you, just made you think I was. Sorry about that. I can almost re-call every trip into the woods, to the dump, and to the race track on the weekends, especially on Sundays. I can almost remember with crystal clarity, everything you've ever taught me, from picking horse's hooves correctly to changing the plug in the lawn mower. Which I still blame you for the bearing mom gave me when the plug went missing and I couldn't start it, and she thought I was being lazy. But it's okay. I survived. It only hurt after the first hit. I want you to know that I was never mad at you, even when you took whatever was wrong out on me, verbally of course. You never hit me unless I asked for it, and I did on several occasions. No hard feelings there. But what I don't understand dad is why. Why did you let mom do what she did to me? I couldn't take a shower except on Sunday, I couldn't brush my own teeth, till I was 16, imagine my breath. The clothes I wore, were hand me downs that were repaired over and over again again. You never said anything why? I really wish you had done more to help me at that time, but I think you were just as scared of her as I was.

But I do Thank You for doing what you did when I was 16. Letting my hair grow, brushing my teeth, wearing better clothes, making friends, letting me out of the house, trying out for the JR baseball team, even though I failed and you knew I would. I can still see your face the day I came home and told you. I think it hurt you as much as it did me. Because instead of chores you let Jeff (my best friend) come over and take me to town for the night, you did all my chores and barn sat the animals till I got home, on top of your 12-hour day at the track, and 8 hours of farm work. Thank You DAD. You always recognized my hard work, even if it was just between us. When I was out in the barn or the fields hours before I had to start my chores, you never asked why. I think you always knew that the farm was actually my escape. While most would run away from chores or delay having to start them, not me, I couldn't wait to get into them. It was my diversion, especially cutting the wood. I had to be so physical, that it helped me handle whatever aggression I had. Boy, did I have some aggression, between mom's constant barrage of insults and anger and all the bullying I had to handle in school I should have been a mess. But I wasn't, you wouldn't let me. You never let me feel sorry for myself, in between the chores, you gave me, small "field trips" into the world. The drive to the really poor section of town to show me there was indeed people worse off than me, under the guise of buying the "best apple pie" in the world off a homeless mom of 5 and then saying you didn't have change and gave her the whole $50.00 sometimes the $100.00. I never knew till later that you paid for the shoes those kids got once a year with money you made at the track at night, being a "catch driver" for the sulky horses at Saratoga. I want you to know I never told mom. Not once. She tried, but I always held my ground. I want you to know I never told her our secrets, the ice cream on the way home on Sundays after working the track all the day, or the sips of whiskey at 16 you let me have while I watched football and you played cards at the drivers club Sundays when we got done early. There were so many little things you did for me. Telling me to bring clothes to school and talking to my gym teacher so I could shower before classes began just so I could fit in. Having Jeff keep a suitcase of "lost" clothes at his house so I would always have clean clothes at school to change into. I lied to you once, and I have regretted that every day of my life. Sorry about that. I chalk it up to youthful desire. I only did it once, for the love of a girl. I think you knew that though. I don't know if I said it enough then, I thought I did but Thank You. You were always, honest, thoughtful, and caring. I can't count how many times I needed money for a date or just to go out. Most kids were lucky to get $10.00. You would reach into the shoe box under the bed and hand me a $50.00 bill, ask me if my chores were done, and if they were, I was all set. The one and only lie evolved from lying about chores so I could go out with a girl. What did you do? You didn't take the money back, or call the girl's father; you added extra chores, ensuring I wasn't going anywhere the next day. Subtle but effective. Never did that again. From the first day we set foot on the farm, and we cleared out first field together, I know we had a ... ? Lack of a better word "connection", for me you were the last shot I had at having a father. When my younger brother, your natural son, backed away from you and broke your heart, and I went out into the barn one night, I climbed out the window to see why the light was on, and found you with a bottle of whiskey crying I know I had to step up. This farm couldn't run itself, and with everyone leaving, and all the problems internally we had as a family, you needed somebody on your side, and I wanted it to be me. My older brother told me I shouldn't, the other one just gave me dirtier looks and walked away. I didn't care, you did your best under unreal circumstances and I was going to make sure you didn't do it alone... Moving on ....

How did all of that craziness, come anywhere near being what I needed to learn about being a man in the world? Easy.... because of you. Everything you did to me, the hard work, the chores, and the personal responsibility for my own belongings, saws, tools etc. All served a purpose. The lessons on how to take down a tree, walk colic off a pregnant mare, kill a rattler in the wood pile, to how not to cut yourself shaving, were all part of what I needed. But most importantly, the lessons you taught about kindness; pulling out a chair for mom, roses on the way home, shoes for strangers, all of this plus countless others gave me the basis for who I am today. Not only for today, but for yesterday and tomorrow. Do you think at 4'11" and 130lbs that I could ever have carried an m-60 strapped to my back, 50lb ammo can in each hand running a mile? Well, I did because of the resolve you taught me to have. Could I have ever had the composure to arrest a 3 star general during a military exercise caring an "outstanding performer" certificate for my efforts?? Not if it hadn't been for you. Introducing me to a lot of people in high places. Well, higher than I was. (Track officials, other owners, riders etc.) You taught me that there is a time and place for everything, when to speak, when to shut up. That knowledge served me well as a student leader in college. Thank You DAD

But the biggest Thank You, I had to save for last. Thank you for always believing in me and never making me feel that I wasn't worth something whenever mom said I was "worthless" and wouldn't amount to doing any better that "selling balloons on a street corner" you always winked and struck your tongue out making me laugh, never allowing the emotions of worthlessness, fortifying my already budding sense of wellbeing. If it hadn't been for that could I have ever found the courage to be married for 31 years, 3 children, 3 grandchildren? I don't think so. Thank you DAD. In the simplest of terms, I am who I am today because of what you did for me. At the time I'm sure it may have seemed like nothing or maybe it was all a part of a plan put in motion by you or it could be just plain dumb luck, either way your way of life, the way you held yourself up, your resolve, your knowledge of the outdoors, your courage, kindness everything that you had and gave to me, really did make all the difference in the world. Without that who knows what path I would have chosen. To this day I use the lessons you taught me to teach others through my umpiring programs for youths to couching youngsters in a pee – wee football league. Dad your lessons were timeless as you were. You were a simple man who believed that the strength of a man's hand shake said more about a man than all the money he had. You believed in a hard day's work, doing whatever it takes to get the job done, and that the real rewards in life are not always easily seen. It is indeed with a heavy heart that I write this to you, but I wanted you to know how grateful I was for everything you did for me. You made me feel like I had a father, and there was nothing you wouldn't do for me. You proved this when I graduated high school and you were the only parent to show up, as mom was busy elsewhere. But it didn't matter, you were there. How dare she ever question why I looked at you like my father because to me you were my father, in every way possible. Everything I am today is because of you. Thank You DAD

I hope I did you proud dad. I hope I didn't disappoint , and I never said enough, but I love you, and I couldn't , wouldn't be here if it hadn't been for you. All I can give back dad is my thanks, and my eternal admiration and Love

Thank You DAD

"Gone But Never Forgotten"

EILEEN DONBECK DOYON

LUDWIKA "LUCY" PRENETA DONBECK

Grandma Lucy as I stood in front of your headstone last year as I had done so many years prior, the dates of your life hit me! 1893-1924..... Oh my God, you were only 31 years young! To my embarrassment, I never realized the time span.

You left behind your husband John, my grandpa, my Aunt Vi, the oldest at age 8 and the only girl, my Uncle Bill, and twins, Uncle Steve and Uncle Louie, and my dad, Johnny, the youngest being only three months old. I knew that you died of pneumonia and had some complications giving birth to my dad.

How your children must have missed you and wanted to know so much about you. Missing Christmases, birthday parties, and just sitting around the dining room table and receiving big hugs. Wanting to know your favorite color, perfume, or having you read their favorite bedtime story. Being 1924, there were not many records or photographs.

I started my quest this year (2014) researching you. I was determined to find out something about you and to answer as many questions as I could.

My dad would always yell at me for running around barefoot outside. I hated wearing shoes or anything on my feet. He would always say, "You are like my mother, she always ran around barefoot." He would laugh and smile. Of course, this is what was told to him growing up.

My dad was in his 70's, Grandma Lucy, before he ever saw a picture of you. I remember him telling me and saying that he just stared at you for hours. The questions and thoughts he must have had. He would have a twinkle in his eye in telling me and must have told me hundreds of times, but I did not mind. I now have two pictures of you that hang on my wall and treasure them dearly. One picture, I think you are about 13 years young, and the other one is a wedding group photo. There is a little girl in the front row that looks just like me. I even had a picture made where I took a picture of me around the same age, four or five, and cannot tell the two apart. I think that is a sign from you thanking me for searching. And who are all the others?????? More searching to do!

Grandma Lucy, I am so much like my dad. We are two peas in a pod and I am daddy's little girl. He was so visual, had unique and different tastes and a style all to his own from the rest of the family. I truly believe that we are like YOU!

My search for information started with my cousins Timmy and Tina. Timmy had a dining room table covered with information he had gathered over the years about you and Grandpa. He has original passports belonging to you both. They are yellowed being made out of paper from the 1800's. There I found your maiden name and that you came from Kupna, a city in Poland. So my search was on its way.

I met a woman named, Patty at The Family History Center in New Hampshire. I think it was not a coincidence in us meeting. She has helped me in my mission immensely. I found out that you arrived in America on October 27th, 1913. The record log book said that you were 19 years young. We think you were younger than that and lied so that you could travel here by yourself to be reunited with your family. So many people at that time came here and settled in America. The rest of the family would follow. Your occupation was listed as a maid, but in reviewing census thru the years, it stated that you were a seamstress and a dressmaker. I believe that is where my dad and I get our creativity from is YOU! How strong willed you were at such a young age to travel by yourself to come to America. You lived in Poultney, VT til you married grandpa the following year in 1914. Your parents lived there, as well as your two sisters. I have been tracking the family tree and found three distant cousins. I have contacted all three and pray that one will answer and have so much information to share with me and even some photographs. I think my determination and stubbornness came from you as well. Please take that as a compliment! Remember, my dad and I are alike and I think we follow in your footsteps!

What stories and life lessons would you have told me growing up? I would have loved to have heard about your travels, what it was like, how you met grandpa? Did you know him from Poland? What were your dreams? What would family dinners have been like with you sitting at the table with us? Grandpa must have missed you dearly. I was told that some relatives wanted to take all the children and raise them cause you were gone. Grandpa kicked them out of your home and he raised the kids by himself.

Grandma Lucy, today now that I am 57 years young, I know that you are with me, guiding me, and helping me find the answers to my questions little by little. I love you dearly and know some day; you will answer all of my questions, and greet me with a big, huge hug!!!! Love you...........

ELIZABETH GARRISON

SARAH ELIZABETH HOVIS GARRISON
May 24, 1935 – December 09, 2005

c/o God, Our Heavenly Father Jesus
In Heaven

Dearest Mom: I never dreamed I would be here on earth without you. There is so much I want to say to you and hug you and feel your arms around me telling me you love me. Since I was born through my years growing up you taking me to Church every Sunday and teaching me about heaven and this is where we all wanted to go when we died but I never thought about the fact one day you, my mother could leave me in this world without your presence, your love, your hugs and your sweetness. I know your life was not everything you deserved. For some unknown reason I thought Dad would leave this earth first and I had plans for you, for us. I wanted you to live with me and take care of you and show you places you had never been. There was so much out in the world you missed and I wanted to share it with you mom. I wanted you to be happy and I wanted you to have it all. Your life was hard. You taught me about commitment to marriage by staying with Dad. You were so selfless. You gave us what we needed and wanted and you chose to go or do without but I did not see your sacrifices until I reached about forty. You were all about family, you had the kindest heart, sweetest smile, morals and most importantly you made us feel loved. I always referred to you as my flower as I matured. You were a fragile and beautiful person and I loved you beyond words. You loved me. You gave me the strength and courage to be what you could not be. You believed in me. I knew you were proud of my successes and that was success for me knowing you were proud of me. In my times of trials and heartaches you comforted me. I knew if I came home just being near you gave me comfort. I felt safe and secure. You were my anchor here on earth.

When we found out you had adenocarcinoma in October 2005 at Sierra Jordan, my youngest daughter's 3rd birthday party and my grandson, Skyler Thomas's 3rd birthday party you arrived with tears yet you tried to hide something was wrong. You chose not to share it with me until after the party was over and only then because I knew something was going on when 2 or 3 show up and obviously had been crying. Mom, I then packed my bags to stay at home with you and Dad and take care of you. I became your strength. I took over trying to help you, understand your feelings and you never let me cry when everyone else could. You told me repeatedly "You have to be strong Elizabeth". I told you I would see you through and I did. I did your makeup and hair when you left and went to heaven. Mom you looked as beautiful as always. Those eight (8) weeks were the shortest weeks of my life. The one thing I couldn't do was give you "time", give me "time". I recall the song "Time In A Bottle" and I wrote it in your card with flowers I kept next to your bed. Coincidently you stated you heard that song that day on the radio. You loved music too.

Mom, this letter is intended to tell you I have tried to do the things for our family as you did. I tried being you. I failed. No one can fill your shoes. I tried to be a grandmother to Thomas's children and Connie's son. I tried making sure Connie had the Christmas gifts you always gave us and no matter what I did I wasn't you. I couldn't make it easy for Connie losing you too. You were the one that held this family together. I miss you so much and I long to come home and hug my little mother but you are not there. I try to stay as close to God's Word for peace and to come home to where you are in Heaven. It is said, Home is where your heart is so being here without you in my worldly life tells me I am in the wrong place. Home is with our Lord and Savior Jesus Christ and where you are. Dad left us in September of 2013 and I pray he found you. I love you

Mom and your love is the only true love I have yet to see or feel unconditionally here.

I'll see you when my purpose here on earth is done for God. Please don't give up on me, I will be there too someday. My work is not complete here. I told Sierra Jordan and Candace Elizabeth, my daughters that God needed Angels and you had been chosen. It was an Honor but you are closer now because you are always in our heart every day and everywhere we travel. I knew Candace would understand but Sierra was only 3. She loved you and had spent every day with you while I worked until you got too sick and I would not let you keep her. Mom we all miss you and nothing has been the same since you left. Our family has withdrawn and it feels like everyone left. Our family longs to be with you again.

With All My Love and Gratitude,

I am thankful and blessed to be called your daughter.

I love you Mom

Elizabeth Ann Garrison

FLYNN GIRLS

JANET FLYNN

CAILYN FLYNN

"When you lose your sense of humor, you lose yourself." Well said by my Father once before.

Following the moment my Grandpa passed away, my Grandma may have lost a lot of heartfelt things. The love of her life, her home in Cape Elizabeth, her stability to walk, and much of her dear memory. The one thing that never left her side was that woman's impeccable sense of humor. She never failed to keep the family smiling and laughing endlessly.

Grandma, I also cannot express how grateful we are for every moral and manner you taught us. I know you will be clapping up there for every time I correct someone's grammar! Heaven has gained one beautiful angel, inside and out. Rest in peace Gram, I love you to the moon and back.

EMILY-ANNE FLYNN

This is a prayer dedicated to my Grandma:

God looked around His garden and found an empty place. He then looked down upon the Earth and saw your tired face. He put his arms around you and lifted you to rest. God's garden must be beautiful- He always takes the best. He saw the road was getting rough and the hills were hard to climb, so he closed your weary eyelids and whispered "Peace be thine." It broke our hearts to lose you but you didn't go alone, for part of us went with you the day God called you home.

Rest in peace Gram I will never forget all the lifelong lessons you have taught me. I love you Gram, and I know you are in a better place watching over everyone who loves you. We will all celebrate your beautiful life!

ALLISON FLYNN

I thought of you with love today, but that is nothing new. I thought about you yesterday and days before that too. I think of you in silence, I often speak your name. All I have are memories and your picture in a frame. Your memory is my keepsake, with which I'll never part. God has you in his keeping; I have you in my heart! Forever and Always

Do Not Stand at My Grave and Weep ~ By Mary Elizabeth Frye

Do not stand at my grave and weep,
I am not there, I do not sleep.
I am in a thousand winds that blow,
I am the softly falling snow.
I am the gentle showers of rain,
I am the fields of ripening grain.
I am in the morning hush,
I am in the graceful rush

Of beautiful birds in circling flight,
I am the star shine of the night.
I am in the flowers that bloom,
I am in a quiet room.
I am in the birds that sing,
I am in each lovely thing.
Do not stand at my grave and cry,
I am not there. I do not die.

"HEAVEN'S GROCERY STORE" ~ Author Unknown

I was walking down life's highway a long time ago.
One day I saw a sign that read,

"HEAVEN'S GROCERY STORE"
As I got a little closer
the door came open wide
And when I came to myself
I was standing inside.

I saw a host of ANGELS.
They were standing everywhere.
One handed me a basket and said,
"My Child shop with care".

Everything a Christian needed
was in that grocery store.
And all you couldn't carry,
you could come back the next day for more.

First, I got some PATIENCE:
LOVE was in the same row.
Further down was UNDERSTANDING:
You need that everywhere you go.

I got a box or two of WISDOM,
a bag or two of FAITH.
I just couldn't miss the HOLY GHOST,

For it was all over the place.

I stopped to get some STRENGTH and COURAGE
To help me run this race.
By then my basket was getting full,
But I remembered I needed some GRACE.

I didn't forget SALVATION,
For SALVATION was free,
So I tried to get enough of that
To save both You and Me.
Then I started up to the counter
To pay my grocery bill,
For I thought I had everything
To do the MASTER'S Will.

As I went up the aisle, I saw PRAYER:
And I just had to put that in,
for I knew when I stepped outside,
I would run into Sin.

PEACE AND JOY were plenty
they were last on the shelf.
SONG and PRAISE were hanging near,
so I just helped myself.

Then I said to the angel,
"Now, how much do I owe?"
He smiled and said,
"Just take them everywhere you go."

Again, I smiled and said,
"How much do I really owe?"
He smiled again and said,
"MY CHILD, JESUS PAID YOUR BILL
A LONG, LONG TIME AGO."

After reading this poem, I couldn't help but smile and think that if there really was a "Heaven's Grocery Store", Grandma would need more than a basket, she would need a cart and even then, the cart would overflow. She brought so much joy to all of us and whenever she was around, she made everything feel vibrant. I think of her in colors often, usually lime green or red because she wore those colors a lot; but also anything bright and happy, because she always made us feel that way. I remember the old house and many memories are so vivid in my mind when I think of her and grandpa. The first image that comes to mind, besides what she looks like, is of the old house in winter. Gram had put really colorful flowers into the snow in front of her house. I just think of that image and think it's the perfect metaphor for how I see my gram; vibrant, happy, and so perfectly herself. The second memory is of mowing that lawn that seemed like it was the size of a desert back when I was a kid. After all the hard work, Gram would make me a sandwich and give me a Pepsi to reward my efforts. Those sandwiches tasted unlike any other I had ever had, in the best of ways. People say that food made by loved ones always tastes the best because it was made with love, well; she made me a firm believer to that theory. She gave a lot of love. The last memory I want to share is the time Gram told me to never to say goodbye to her. I was young when she said that and confused because that's what you say to people when you leave. She told me not to say goodbye because we will always see each other again, it always needs to be, "so long for now". I remember leaving her house in a car full of kids that didn't want to leave and watching her wave to us until we were long gone. She always did that. She waved until she couldn't see the car anymore. I see my Dad do that sometimes when I leave for school or for a long trip and I immediately think of Gram and how she has affected us all in different ways, for the better.

Recently I've been thinking about where she is and it has been comforting to me to know that she was a woman of good faith. She will be missed but I know she is with us through the stories we tell each other, through the mannerisms we have picked up because of her, and also in spirit. We love you Gram, this is only so long for now.

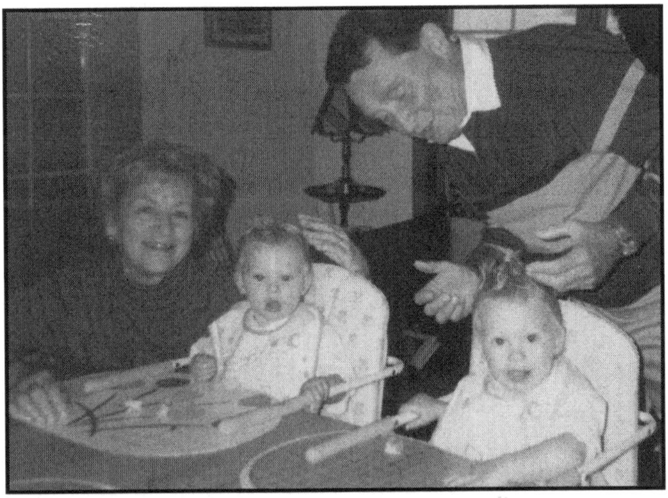

FRAN TUNNO

ROBERT TUNNO

My father's name was Robert Tunno. He passed away at 97, after what we believe was a stroke. I was 57 when he died.

Dear Dad,

When I walked in your door, there was a feeling that came over me I can only describe as calm. When I was with you, I felt a calmness wash over me because we had such a connection. I could sit and talk with you for hours because we knew each other's hearts.

But, because you understood me so well, I think I probably didn't tell you things I should have because, honestly, it felt like you already knew.

I don't think I ever said thank you for letting us move in with you after my divorce. Thank you for being there at the door when I showed up and fell apart, crying in your arms. Even though you were 95 and I was 55, you made me feel protected and loved when I really needed it.

I am embarrassed that even though you opened your home to me, I was feeling sorry for myself. Poor me, I'm divorced, poor me, I don't have my pretty home; it was all about poor me, until I realized you were probably not thrilled to have your home invaded and rearranged by me, my two teenagers and two dogs with tiny bladders.

I want you to know that you saved us and were much more help to us at that time than I know we were to you.

Whatever cooking, cleaning, or chores I did could hardly repay offering your lovely home to us when we needed a place to land, so thank you Dad. And thank you, most of all, for being a wonderful friend to me.

We ended up staying longer than I thought. My hopes of buying a home were ruined by the recession and my ex's credit disasters.

The next year your health began to fail, so there was more reason to stay. You needed more and more help. I was so glad to finally be able give back to you after all your years of giving to me.

You handed me my sweetest memory of our time together. I started helping you get settled at night. At 96 it wasn't easy getting in and out of bed anymore, so every night I helped, just like you helped me when I was little.

You lay in bed, in your thin, light green cotton pajamas, tolerating me fixing your blankets. Night after night, when I leaned over to give you a goodnight kiss on your forehead, you looked up at me with such gratefulness in your eyes, and said, "I don't know what I would do without you."

Unfortunately you found out, because I realized I had to leave. My son moved out months before, and my daughter needed a better high school than the one in our tiny hometown. I wanted her to attend one with better academics, where she'd grown up and known everyone. She deserved that after all she'd been through.

And I needed to go back where I had connections, because my career had stalled. I didn't want to leave you, but sadly, I had to choose between taking care of you and taking care of my daughter.

You were angry with me for leaving you at first, and I don't blame you. I probably would have felt the same. But a month later, you forgave me and understood why I had to go. Thank you for forgiving me.

Your other kids completely picked up where I left off and between them and amazing caregivers; you had round the clock attention. I hope they tucked you in too.

In our last phone conversation, I told you my kids and I would be home for spring break and that I would be seeing you soon. You could hardly hear, had a hard time speaking, and couldn't remember things very well, but of course, you asked if I needed money for plane tickets. Nothing stopped you from wanting to help, but you'd already helped more than you ever knew.

Then you fell ill a week before we were to come home. You lay silent for three days as we took turns sitting with you, holding your hand, to make sure you didn't meet death alone. You took your last breath with your family all around you, in the home you built, where you created a lifetime of sweet memories.

Your example taught me so much Dad: the importance of hard work, how to raise kids and grandkids, how to be a friend, the value of kindness and generosity, and even the art of dying. I know I'll never fill your shoes, but I'll never stop trying.

And now it's my turn to say; "What will I do without you?" I wonder every day how I'll get along without you to talk to. You were so much more than a dad; you were a true friend; cheering me on when I succeeded, and catching me when I fell.

There isn't a day that goes by that I don't miss you and your steady reliable voice saying, "Keep going, you gotta work hard, you can do it. You'll get there."

When I get there, and I plan to, just know, I could never have done it without you.

Love, Frances
AtFransTable.Wordpress.com

GAIL THOMPSON ROBERTSON

LAVERN THOMPSON

In Loving Memory of Lavern Thompson 12/3/1925 – 03/29/1997

Dear Dad,

We knew time was getting close and we would be losing you to the cancer you battled for the past six months. As my birthday approached, I prayed not to lose another person on a day that was special for me. Grandpa had passed on my 20th birthday and I never quite accepted the fact that what was once a day of joy now had become a day of dread. But, pray as I might, you passed away in the early morning hours of March 29, 1997, my 46th birthday. Consequently, that day is still celebrated but it never passes without me shedding tears for the two men that were my first loves of my life and my role models.

Since your passing, so many things have occurred. Most were joyous events but there have been bumps along the way. Things that we wished you were here to celebrate and others to offer your encouragement and sound advice.

On December 24, 1997, you were blessed with another grandchild, Carrie Ann, born to Dave and Theresa. You would have enjoyed watching her grow into the beautiful young lady she is today. Like you, she is quite a swimmer, competing on a swim team from the age of 6.

Your eldest grandchild, Shawn, married and divorced nine years later. So many times he wished his Grandpappy was here to talk to and help him through an emotionally difficult time. You were the one person he could open up to and he knew you would offer sage advice. The good thing that came from that union was your great grandson, Seth. Seth is so much like his father and I can envision you teasing and bantering back and forth with him. Shawn has a new love in his life, Jen. His life is good but would be perfect if he could get custody of Seth.

Your other granddaughter, Amy, is also divorced. She had two children, Colton and Aubrianna. She too is happy in a new relationship with Andy. They have a son, Zachary.

Mom has done quite well and thinks of you daily. She has never remarried or dated. She says that she had the best and no one could live up to that. At 82, she has now lived 11 years longer then you.

In 2004, I was diagnosed with breast cancer. There were times I wondered if I, too, would succumb to cancer. Everyone commented on how strong I was and how well I handled it. Once again, I attribute that to my role model. I watched you endure what you did; never complaining and always proclaiming that we shouldn't be sad because you had a good life. Even to the end you were looking out for us and helping us to accept the inevitable.

I recently had some of your old movie reels converted to CD format. We have enjoyed watching and reminiscing about family and old times. I have had 30 copies made for other family members. Mom said, "Wouldn't your Dad be surprised how far those movie reels have come and how many have enjoyed them!" So, even gone, you continue to touch lives and make an impact. Which is no surprise because family and friends always said and still remember you as a person with a loving, giving heart.

Spring will soon be here. It was always your favorite season because things came back to life. If only you could come back, for even a day, there would be so much to say. With Spring comes March once again and my heart will grow heavy. As I shed my tears on the 29th. Some are for sadness and some for happiness.

Sadness for the loss of a wonderful father and grandfather. Happiness for all the memories of having you for 46 years. Happiness for all you were and all you did for family.

Love, Gail Thompson Robertson

I wish heaven had
visiting hours

JEANNE BUESSER

CARL

Dear Dad,

A long time ago when I was a teenager you tried to instill in me the following lesson. "Think before you speak". At that time I really didn't listen and didn't understand what you were telling me. It wasn't until I was much older that I understood your wisdom and began to listen. Thank you for teaching me to put my thoughts on hold before speaking them. So I wouldn't hurt others by what I said. I wanted to thank you too because you made me look at life through your gentle spirit. I didn't always understand your ways. I never really told you but I was always so amazed and proud to be your daughter. Even now that you're gone I am not only beginning to see what you accomplished in your life by what you left behind. Now I know why I loved the poem by Ralph Waldo Emerson so much and tried to follow it during my life." Do not follow where the path leads, Rather go where there is no path and leave a trail!" Love Jeanne

Dad,

what can I say, to a man like you, a father, friend and teacher too.

Who has taught me much, but so much more for me to learn,

As life like a carousel does turn,

With ups and downs as it spins around, you were there to pick me up off the ground.

But through it all, I've got to say, I wouldn't want it any other way,

I can say with pride, that I hope, and pray, with your health

another 20 years more like today.

You'll still be working on many projects big and small, soon hopefully

finish them all.

Like I said in that turtle figure saying many years ago, "I'm slow but I'm coming"

but I'll get there so,

Keep on walking, doing, never stop yearning and learning,

For life is one big carousel turning!

Happy 80th Birthday Dad!!!!

Jeanne

President, Apraxia Network

Author,Poet, He Talks Funny

Journey From Darkness To Light

Moonlight Till Dawn

www.jeannebuesser.com

www.apraxianetwork.org

JEANNE TROMBLEY

HELEN LESZCZYNSKI KITCHNER

July 2, 1921 - September 12, 2002

Mom, it's been 12 long years since we last talked. I wasn't ready to say goodbye to you, I needed you and I still do. Hardly a day went by that we didn't talk. Funny, if by chance two days went by and you didn't hear from me, the next time we talked you would always say, "well, where have you been?" and then you would have that special laugh that I can still hear...makes me smile.

Deirdre is all grown up now and a mother herself. I have the most beautiful grandson Raymont, AKA "Pee Wee" and "Ray Ray" who was born on April 5, 2012. Mom, you would just love him, he is amazing! I never thought I would ever fall in love again. I see a lot of Timmy in him when he was his age; it's the cheeks, so pudgy. They both lived here for nearly two years but she is now on her own. I loved the time I had with him here and playing such an important role in his life as a baby, taking care of his every need. I cherished every minute of it. I also had the chance to instill some of my ways, which I inherited from you, and pass on to him. I want him to experience some of the simple things in life like I had as a child. My stepson Jeremy is married now to a wonderful woman, Angelica and I have two grandbabies, Landon and Arilyn. Sadly they live in Georgia so I don't see nearly enough of family. I want to say you can't imagine how I feel but of course you do, you had nine grandbabies.

The log house was finally finished and I started living here in 2003. I'm so glad you had the opportunity to see the property I purchased and the view of the lake I have. Your china cabinet sits in the dining room corner with all your fancy dishes on display. It was meant to be here with me. Your table is in my dining room as well. Oh, and the blue glass cross that hung over my bed is one of my fondest keepsakes of yours. I look around my home and I see you everywhere as with my garden.

Dick's Mom passed away in July 2013 and days after Dick was diagnosed with cancer. It was a rough year for all of us. He went thru several months of chemo and radiation treatments along with several hospital stays. One year later he is cancer free and enjoying life once again.

I retired from the County last January after 37 years. What a summer I had, best since I began working. So relaxing, slow paced and time for me to really do what I love most, yard work. Mom, I have your green thumb and always have a very productive garden. I listened and learned it all from you. Gardening is one of my favorite outlets in life…I think of you all the time when I'm planting it, tending to it, processing it and best of all, eating it! My latest chapter in life, I started a new job in December at a pharmacy in Greenwich. I really enjoy the job and the change of pace from what I have done for so many years.

Mom, there are some things I wish I had said to you but never did. So, I want you to know…Number one, you were not only my mother but you were the best friend I ever had. And you were such a strong woman growing up with little of nothing. I admire your braveness the way you battled lung cancer, bladder cancer, kidney cancer and heart disease. I never told you how much I loved you, admired you. Your determination and courage to face all these obstacles with the most positive attitude and determination inspires me. You always said life was a gift of God.

Mom, I hope this letter finds its way to you in heaven. I love and miss you.

KITCHNER

JENN SCHAAFF

GARY MUCHA

December 25, 1951 - November 3, 2005

It was 9 years ago today; you called me on my cell as I was driving your first born grandson to his first photo session for his baby pictures. I pulled over on the side of the road to talk to you. You were a little out of breathe, I asked if you were doing ok – that is when you said "Jenn, honey, I'm dying". I tried to be positive (as usual) and say no, you weren't you were probably just a little tired from walking outside. Sit down and take a rest at Grandpa's and I will call you later to check on you. You said "no honey, really this time I am dying". My eyes were teary already and I started to cry. You told me not to get upset because then the baby would (he was 6 weeks old). I mumbled ok Daddy, I will try to stay calm, but I love you and will see you tomorrow. I have off with the baby and we will come down after his 6 week checkup and you & Grandpa can meet him for the first time. You said-ok honey that sounds good. I love you and you will be a wonderful Mom I know you will, your mom was for you. As I was crying a little uncontrollably now, I said I love you too Daddy and thank you, I will try my best.

The next morning, I got up and got ready for the day, took my baby (Freddy IV) to the doctor's for his checkup. He was growing and doing well, perfect in my eyes! It turned out after his appointment I had to go to work, so I took Freddy to the sitters and went to work. On my way in my Grandpa called my cell but I couldn't answer it. So I called him back as soon as I got to work. Grandpa hardly ever called so I knew it was something important. I called Grandpa and he said ...."honey, Daddy passed this morning". I screamed...yelled...cried and turned to my cube mate, she asked if I was ok. I recall yelling "no my Dad died!!! "

I told Grandpa I would call my husband and we would get the baby and go right down. I could hear he was choked up and maybe crying - this is a man I have never seen cry in all my life. He said please drive carefully.

I was so upset, my cube mate had to talk to my husband, and I couldn't even talk all I could do was cry and hyperventilate. Finally my coworkers were able to help me calm down. When my husband got to work we called my sitter and told her the news, she said not to worry about the baby she would take care of everything, and then went straight down to Grandpa's. We decided it would be a little easier for me to comprehend what had just happened if I didn't have to worry about the baby too. My sitter was fabulous and kept the baby overnight for us. We got down to Grandpa's and stayed a while to console him. Once he saw me he broke down.

After your services and things had calmed down a little I went down every weekend with the baby to see Grandpa. He really enjoyed seeing him and watching his only great-grandson grow up. I took Grandpa and the baby over to see Nan in the nursing home almost every time we went down, we told her of your passing and though she shook her head I'm not sure she really understood. Alzheimer's had set in pretty bad so she was in bed most of the time when we went. Grandpa was the only one who could get her to eat and it was only a banana, but at least it had good vitamins in it for her to try and keep her going.

There were many days that I took time off from work to take Grandpa to his Cancer treatments. One day in particular his visit was at the hospital and as we were about to leave he said he had to use the men's room. So the nurse showed him where it was. He was taking a particularly long time...so the nurse and I walked down the hall to check on him. This was the scariest thing I had encountered at his visits. He was just standing there looking in the mirror. I started talking to him with the door cracked open; he looked at me and said I don't know why I am here. I proceeded to tell him he was in the men's room and asked if he had to go to the bathroom or not. This was a man of dignity and pride and would never want his granddaughter to see him indecent, however the man needed help. So, I guess it was my new motherly instincts that kicked in. We got through all of that just fine and I got him back into the room and told the nurse what just happened. She said it sounded like he had a stroke or something. So......we were now obligated to running more tests to find out what happened. Several hours later, come to find out he did in fact have a "mini stroke" aka TIA.

After that episode I didn't let Grandpa too far out of my site. I took him to every doctor appointment that I could, even got in trouble at work a time or two, but to me family is everything and family comes first. Since my biological side of my family was deteriorating very quickly I did what I had to do and choose family over career and took as much time as I had to.

Thankfully I have the best and most supportive husband in the world who has stood beside me through everything that happened from the birth of our son to the death of you, your father and your mother – that is my entire biological family within 4 years.

Now our son is 9 and boy is this an interesting yet fun age. He is big into hunting thanks to his dad who has taught him everything he could possible learn since he could walk. He is what we call a sharp shooter at 9. He is "dead on balls accurate" (as you would say). We are starting to get to the point in his life where I find myself saying "my Dad taught me that too"....such as how to drive a tractor down a long dirt road and how to stack wood.

There are so many memories that I have from when I was young, but not many from my teen years. I know that is the time at which we drifted apart, mostly because I was pretty rebellious and thought I could do whatever I wanted, whenever I wanted and to whomever I wanted. Had I known then what I know now, I would have realized you were always there for me and had my back when it came to everything. You never shied away, you never gave up, and because of that, we got our friendship back in my early 20's and for that I am forever thankful.

I am glad I was able to be there when you were in the hospital so many times, and I was the one who was contacted when you were sick and driving erratically on the highway only because you were trying to come see your grandson. I am glad I was the one you called every Sunday around 2 in the afternoon just to chat and see how the week was going and how I was adjusting to motherhood and to get your advice on what to do for the baby.

I am glad I was the last person you called and that I answered the phone to talk to you, even if I was driving...LOL! I am glad that we had such a great father daughter relationship at the end that I can carry on and tell my son about as he gets older.

They say everything happens for a reason, and I strongly believe that. My thought has always been you chose the day of the baby's 6 week check up to pass, because you knew he was healthy and you knew I had him to take care of and focus on . Although your passing will never get easy for me, I have realized it was the best for you due to all the illness, pain and suffering you had endured over the last few years. It was time for you and me to move on with our lives.

Not a day goes by that I don't think of you Dad, I love you forever and always. Until we meet again!

Rest In Peace – Gary Mucha December 25, 1951 - November 3, 2005

Jenn Schaaff , CCMT

Pampered Paws K9Massage

KAREN FRANCO

SHARON BENKO

My mom died on May 10, 2005 and she was 67 years old. In 1985, my mom was diagnosed with breast cancer. She went into remission for over 20 years, but then cancer started appearing in other places...her uterus, her liver and finally ended up in her brain. I was 39 years old.

Dear Mom,

There isn't a day that goes by that I don't think of you. How many times I reach for the phone to tell you something or ask you a question, but then I realize I can't. That's how much you are a part of my day...my life. I find myself talking to you in the hopes that you might answer me back.

How did you do it all so gracefully? You were a loving wife, mother, friend, business person and without fail kept everything together. Mom you made each of us feel special and that wasn't always easy with four kids. You were the "glue" for our family. We pulled together and held each other up in every situation. We learned that from you...to always be there for each other no matter what. You always gave us support and told us we could achieve anything. I was looking through old photos and I came across a card that you gave me. I'm so glad that I kept it. The card read..."You can! Whatever you're faced with you can handle. Whatever you're feeling you can cope. Whatever you fear, you can conquer, as long as you believe in yourself...as much as I believe in you.

I remember you always wanted to have a house full of kids...well you had four, but our friends loved spending time at our house so I guess, you really did have a house full of kids. I think that says a lot about the person you were and the fact that our friends wanted to be there. I remember you making big breakfasts on Saturday morning after we had our friends sleep over... I don't think I ever saw you smile more.

You were taken from us far too soon...you had so much of your life to live, but cancer wouldn't let you. Mom, I have never met another person as strong and as brave as you were facing your illness. You never complained or gave up. Mom, you faced your illness with positive thoughts, and you did fight it for so long, but then one day you said that you couldn't do this anymore and that you were tired. It was then that I realized you needed some peace...a place where there wasn't any pain or suffering. It wasn't easy letting you go, but we all knew it was time. Mom you have four wonderful children who loved you and still do with all their hearts.

Everyone you met you touched their heart and you are never forgotten. You were the person that walked into a room and it lit up with laughter and smiles. Your personality, your joy for life, your beauty inside and out is what made you the special woman that you were and will always be for so many people...not just family. I remember Dad saying, "If it wasn't for your mother, I wouldn't have gotten half the jobs that I did. She was smart and savvy and always knew the right things to say to win that customer." When I see your friends, the first thing they mention is your love for cooking. They talk about your wonderful recipes, and how you and dad loved to entertain. No one wanted to miss your parties.

It's funny, I can still hear you singing, and when I hear your favorite song, that's when I know you are with me. Jacob still remembers "your song" that was so special to him when you sang it. He says, "That's Gamma's song," and he smiles. Then I ask him, "Where is Gamma?" He always replies, "She is living with angels." I think that was the best way I could explain to him where you had gone. It isn't easy telling a child with special needs about sickness and passing away especially when his favorite person in the whole world won't be singing to him anymore. My explanation had to be simple and something he could understand in his own way, and I truly believe he does.

Mom, so much has happened to me since you've left us. I can't believe that this year you will be gone for 10 years. It feels like yesterday. You knew that Chris and I were getting married, and we did in September of 2005. We built a beautiful home on Chris' property. I know you would've loved the peace and serenity where we live. Jacob graduated from high school! His ceremony was the most wonderful day for me...just one moment of normalcy. Jake was with his friends in his cap and gown, grinning from ear to ear, he walked across the stage and yelled, "I did it!" That day was one of my proudest moments. I know you were there with him holding his hand the entire time. Since you've been gone, I've become a children's book author. My first book is titled, "Just Hold My Hand," and my second book is "Jacob's Hoop." It's the beginning of a series of books about Jacob's journey in his special needs world. Mom, I can't begin to tell you how excited I am about this chapter in my life. I really enjoy sharing my stories. I just wish I could've shared them with you.

I know in my heart you are always with me...please don't ever leave. Mom, your grace gives me the strength to handle life's situations in the most loving way and I will forever hold onto that.

I love you and miss you,

Your Daughter Karen

Visit my website: www.karenfrancobooks.com

Like me on Facebook: www.facebook.com/karenfrancobooks

KATHY DUNN

RICK JACOBS

Died July 23, 2010 age 65 of sudden coronary event. I was 39 when Rick passed.

Dear Rick,

This year marks the 5th year since your sudden and unexpected passing. The call from my brother while I was right in the middle of moving was met with HUH? What? This is not funny! How could this be? While my brother tried to console me over the phone he told me the lesson most learned from you in his life which was not to leave anything on the table. How true to how you lived your life.

I was very much looking forward to catching up with you in my new house once I got back. You and I talked about meeting and checking out my new place. We last saw each other a few months back and talked quite a bit about our lives which were in similar places. We could talk to each other about so many things which included some tough times. You were my faux 'Uncle Ricky' that came in to my life through my step-father. His best friend and brother in life. You became my friend, my confidante, my roommate once, and someone who was a lot like me and going to the beat of our own drum.

I learned so much about living life through you. Your stories were always legendary and the storyteller just made it even better. The importance of getting a story from an experience has stuck with me and is my goal in everything I do. It's not about the eggs on a plate for breakfast...it is how you get to a 200 dollar bill for breakfast and the story that comes from that.

I have such peace about living my life to the beat of my own drum and know it is perfectly okay. I have my own path that works for me and what is important is that I found it. Like you the nieces and nephews in my life are the best thing that has ever happened to me. To have these loves to spend time with, take on adventures, and teach them the importance of getting their own stories is the best! Nothing is better than seeing them seek out their own experience and to tell the story. I hope when the kids wonder what to do in life they think WWKD- What would (aunt) Kathy do?

I have such moments that I wish I could still be sharing with you. Indeed you would have loved my new place. I finally met your protégé, Sammy, and could see why you got along so well. I think of you during Patriots games and how you would not come during the cold games with me. I think of that first night you took up temporary residence at my house and sticking your hand over the fire pit to only yelp out...."WHOA! That's hot! No kidding Rick. Oh and that dolphin...priceless.

One night you appeared in my dreams. The dream was so vivid. You came to see me to borrow a camera as you were going on a trip and would be gone for a while. You came to say good-bye to me. I remember waking up and feeling this burden had been lifted from me. You didn't forget me and came to say good-bye... in our own way of course.

May God bless and keep you always

May your wishes all come true

May you always do for others

And let others do for you

May you build a ladder to the stars

And climb on every rung

May you stay forever young

Forever young, forever young

May you stay forever young.

Miss you Rick. Until we meet again. Rock on.

Love,
Kathy

Kathy Dunn
Hampton Beach, NH

KATHERINE CARLSON-PENLEY

MARIE SANTOSUOSSO

To Our Lovely Marie,

Daughter, Sister, Mother, Grandmother, Aunt, Sister-in-Law, Animal Lover, Friend.

When I received the text message last year of your test results, time stood still. Emotions of confusion flooded my thoughts trying to grasp the word that every human avoids – Cancer. It's a word that people want to stay away from; it's a word that is frightening and confusing. You brought our families together one night to talk about Cancer and to learn the expectations of what will come in the following months. You were given one year. One year to cram as much of life as you possibly can by creating and completing your bucket list. You brought us together to talk about our feelings whether it was sadness, happiness, fear, anger. It was your wish to ask every family member to open their hearts to accept your illness, to accept this frightening reality, to begin your journey of your Life's End.

I'm going to miss you, Marie. I already miss you. I miss our talks, our gossips, our dreams that we shared, your love of dragonflies. I already miss planning my Saturday drives to your home in Saugus, Massachusetts, to make homemade scrapbook gifts in shadow boxes and pictures frames. You told me who is to receive a gift and to show them to everyone at your funeral before handing them over to the family members. By your wish, I have brought them here to the church today. I want to text message you when arriving in Saugus asking if you still want a Dunkin Donuts Regular Iced Coffee – Medium or Large. Of course, the choice was always large. I want to see you zip through Sam's Club again driving the electronic cart while shopping for food items with Ma and me for our annual summer party. I want to hear your laughter again and to see your most beautiful angelic blue eyes when you say, 'WHATEVAH!'

I am beginning to come to grips that these moments with you will not come true anymore but the memories of our time together is everlasting. I only knew you for 10 years when I began dating your brother, Brian, and when we got to know each other more, we found that we share a few similarities. We are the only daughter in our own families with two brothers as siblings AND we both are the middle child. We both talked about what it would have been like to have a sister growing up and when you and I found each other, our wish came true. We talked about how love, life and family have special moments and we talked about little secrets that only sisters are allowed to know. We talked about our dreams where our grandmothers would visit us during the nights to give encouragement about being strong and that everyone will be okay. A special bond indeed.

I remember sharing with you a dream I had years ago after recovering from my automobile accident and what kind of affect it had on me. This dream was in the late 1990s and you and I did not meet until the year 2004. It was a dream about my friend's wife who was dying from a long illness of cancer. I was in a circle with a few women including Janice, the wife of my friend, sitting on what appeared to be white clouds moving in a slow rotation but it did not feel like the clouds were moving. We were all in white silk gowns and we were busy talking and laughing while sewing together the most silkiest of white silk fabric with white feathers. The fabric endlessly wrapped around, over and beneath us and was also within our circle. The feel of the fabric and feathers were so light that when it was touched, it was the softest and calmest creation I had ever felt. I was allowed to join them only for a few minutes before returning to my life and waking up from a night's sleep. After two days, Janice passed away. After I spoke of this dream, you said that we were making Angels' Wings and I said, 'Yes, we were'. But what I did not tell you and what I realized at that moment is that one of the Wings would be yours.

There is another dream that I had a few days before you and Dean renewed your wedding vows. I chose not tell you this dream until after your journey on Earth ended. It's a dream that epitomizes a celebration of life. I was in a very long line meeting people I did not recognize until I saw my Guardian Angel, my maternal grandmother, Leona Bowden. She was in a very long line walking opposite of me. When I saw her, I grabbed her tightly telling her I missed her so much and that I did not want her to leave me. But she released our hug, smiled and said, 'Be Strong'. My grandmother had the most beautiful smile and angelic sky blue eyes that always drew me to her. Fear was coming forth where I tried walking towards her but she was gone and strangers continued walking the long lines. The room was majestic much like a royal Victorian ballroom and I remember many people wore Victorian gowns and tuxedos; others wore regular clothes. The walls of the room were adorned with gorgeous hand-painted art from the bottom to the high ceilings with hundreds of carefully crafted white pillars.

You and Dean decided to renew your wedding vows after 27 years of marriage and the date was scheduled for June 07, 2014. One month before, you, Ma and I went to Dave's Bridal to try on wedding gowns and when you had the fourth gown on, you said, 'This is it'. You kept referring to the gown as your Princess Gown. And it truly was a gown especially made for you – our Princess. When you asked me to be your Maid-of-Honor, I felt blessed to be part of your special day with you and Dean. Preparing for your wedding was a special time from countless trips to Michael's Craft Store to refitting appointments at Dave's Bridal to scratching our heads drawing up a floor plan for the reception room using a small notepad with quarters wondering where to place tables, chairs, buffet tables and a dance floor. June 7th came and your wedding was beautiful with magical moments of love, laughter, and family that will stay within us forever.

This past Tuesday, 08/26/2014, your journey ended with us and now your own journey to everlasting love, laughter and life begins. You have already taken the wings made for you and have begun your work. After we left your house that evening, Brian and I stopped at our favorite restaurant, Border Café, to have dinner. When it was time to pay the bill, we started talking to our waiter who introduced himself as Taylor. After we told him we were regulars and how we love the food and service, he spoke how he decided to work here because he loved the French Quarter Chicken. Brian told me this was your favorite item at the restaurant where he used to stop here to pick up French Quarter Chicken to bring to you. We were both stunned. Brian shared with Taylor of your passing earlier that day and how you loved this food item. We told him we will always ask to sit at one of his tables from now on. He was very grateful........ but.......... I think you already knew that.

Marie, your guests in the ballroom are waiting for you. I realize now that the hundreds of people in the majestic Victorian ballroom is your grand finale. Your family and friends have brought their guests and they are all in long reception lines waiting to see you in your Princess Gown. There is an Old Path that you will find which will lead you to this place. Once you are there, it will be Home. But knowing you, I'm sure you will stop at Rainbow Bridge to pick up your beloved four-legged furry friends including a gazillion dragonflies because, as a Sister, you cannot go to a party without holding onto something. This is your time but it is also our time to reflect your kindness, your love, and your strong sense of courage in being The Rock for the Penley and Santosuosso Families. For us who are still here on Earth, it is now our turn to be The Rock, to help each other heal and continue on with our lives until the day we will be with you again. Your heart touched many, many people as shown on Facebook and the explosion of messages continue on.

Fly High, My Loving Sister and Friend. I will miss you dearly.

With Much Love from your Sister-In-law,

Katherine Carlson-Penley

8/29/2014

KIMMY LUCAS

FRANCIS X LUCAS

DIED 1974 AGE 51

Dear Daddy, How I miss to be held by you. The morning I was woken up from Linda, telling me you died, I felt my whole world turn upside down. I wasn't sure why my sister was at my side so early in the morning. I was very confused of your absence to my life. I had just lost my Daddy at age 11, forever. I will never forget how much you loved me. Holding your hand, sitting on your lap, or on your hip, in your arms feeling safe and protecting me as Daddies should. Watching you as a Fireman for our Town, and going to special Events at the Firehouse, always made me so very proud and special. I loved walking through the fields by our house with you to go home after spending a day at the Fire House. You always treated Michael, Lisa and Me to Sam's Soda Fountain Candy Store. A memory none of us, will never forget. I loved to see you hug Mommy when you came home from a hard day's work, at the Court House. Taking Michael, Mommy, and me away on vacations was always fun. Visiting family from the East Coast, Down South, and then through to the West Coast. One of my favorite spots was seeing my Cousin Dale in Mississippi. :):) Also seeing my siblings we visited. I always missed them, as they all moved away when I was so young. I have never forgotten my 6th grade Graduation dance with you. I had the chance to have my dance with my Daddy. A moment for me, a moment frozen in time! Being daddy's little girl and not having you here has been so very hard on me. At times I miss you so dearly, I drop to my knees and ask God why he took you away from me. You gave me such beautiful qualities within myself. Patriotism, Family, Respect, Honor, Loyalty, and Love. I have now passed on these beautiful qualities to my 3 Children, Kristy, Vincent and Ericca, your Grandchildren. And in return, we will continue to pass down to all the next generations. I know you would be so proud. I feel you watching over me and guiding me with the hands that once protected and held me safe. Till our hearts and hands meet again, I will forever miss you Daddy. With loving arms, your little girl Kimberly Anne xoxo

Bottom row, 2nd from left

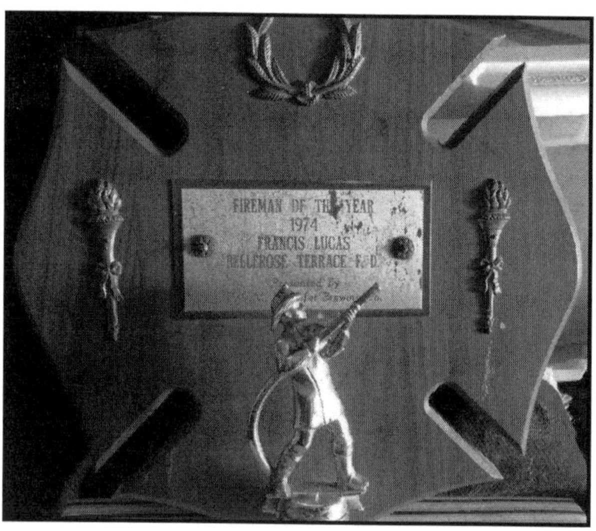

As I sit here and whisper,
"I miss you"
I believe somehow
you can still hear me.

KIRSTEN LARSEN SCHULTZ

ROBERT ETHER

If I could write one letter to heaven, I would chose to write to my Grandfather to fill him in on the important events in my life that he's missed since he's been gone. Not having a father figure in my life, my Grandfather was a central figure in my childhood and early adult years until his passing in 2001. His last years were difficult as the Alzheimer's stole his memory and he did not appear to recognize us. At the time I was living in the south pursuing a career in auto racing but shortly after his death returned to NH to be closer to home and family with a renewed appreciation for the brevity of life and the importance of family relationships over job and money.

At his memorial service I was honored to speak about my Grandfather, who he was and what he meant to me.

> It has been told to me, and so the story goes: When my mom told her dad that he was to become a grandfather for the first time the stoic marine responded with "I am not going to be poohpa, papa, umpa or any of the sort" and so it was and he was not. A tiny little girl looked up at her grandfather and uttered "Grandfather" for the first time.
>
> My grandfather was truly a great grandfather. I remember when he took Timothy, Joel, and I on our first train ride - all the way to Fort Edward. I remember him taking me to the

top of the Empire State Building and looking out over New York City for the first time.

He taught me how to play basketball and to fish. We often went out on the lake, just the two of us, to catch fish. I had to bait my own hook of course, but he would take the fish off for me. I remember the time I got the fish hook stuck in my thumb. He calmly pulled it out, stuck my hand in the water to clean it off, and told me to suck on it to ease the pain and stop the bleeding. You never had a chance to be afraid because you always felt save and cared for with him.

Grandfather even took me to my first stock car race in Malta. It was probably because Uncle Jim wanted to go, but still he took us, and I am sure he had no idea at the time what the future would have in store for me.

As I got older, he filled me with knowledge. He had an explanation for everything you might ever want to know about and even some things that you didn't care to know at the time. I remember in minute detail the lesson on the inner workings of a transmission and a clutch.

When I was visiting from North Carolina in the summer of 1989 and became sick and wanted to go home, Grandfather put me in the car the next morning at 6 am and we began the non-stop drive back to Charlotte. We didn't make many pit stops and sure got there quick, even in time to bring home a pizza to mom for dinner.

When I went off to college and other students had posh dorm room setups with lofts, he was quick to make one and stuff it in the trunk of his Sentra to personally deliver and install it. And on my 18th birthday he presented me with this necklace with the following message: "Dear Kirsten; when grandfather was eighteen years old, he found this on the beach of Eniwetok Atoll in the Marshall Islands. He decided to save it for a very special person. You are that person! I Love You, Grandfather." At the time I didn't realize how special this is, but I do now.

He might not have said "I Love You" often, yet I always knew that I held a very special place in his heart. To this day he is my loving Grandfather. He will not be there to walk me

> down the aisle on my wedding day as I had always hoped. But I know that he is in a much better place and that for the rest of my life, until we meet again in heaven, I will have a very special guardian angel with me, taking care of me, watching out for me, just as he always has.

Grandfather, so many important moments have happened in my life since you left us in 2001 but I know that you've been my guardian angel every day. For years I wondered when the right one would come along, doubted if he ever would, but I knew that you were up there searching to find just the right partner for me. I often would picture you standing beside God pointing down to earth and saying "No, that one won't do", "Hmmm, maybe that one, no, not good enough for my little girl." They say that a girl marries someone like her father, but for me, I know it was to be someone like my Grandfather. I knew you'd never meet him but somehow you still had to approve. I became friends with Shawn in 2005 although it wasn't until 2008 that we started dating. He is a lot like you. He is always tinkering with and fixing things and will not give up until he figures it out. Like you, Shawn doesn't wear his emotions on his sleeve, yet I always know he loves me. We were married in August 2011. Uncle Jim stood in for you to walk me down the aisle and I could feel your presence smiling down on us.

I never really expected to be a mom but in April 2013 we welcomed our daughter Cathryn Jae, named after Grandma. It was heartwarming to see Grandma's tears of joy when we told her we were naming our daughter after her. CJ, as we have come to call her, is full of life, a thirst for knowledge and brings us great joy. I know you always wanted to see Grandma become a great-grandmother and now she is (times three!) I only wish that you had a chance to know Cathryn Jae and that she had a chance to know her great grandfather.

Our family has grown with marriages and the birth of a new generation, but we are not the same in your absence. You were the core that kept us all together. I know that one day we will all be together again and you will meet Shawn and Cathryn Jae. I look forward to that day so much - perhaps once again we can take the boat out on the lake - just you and I - and catch up on all the things that have happened in my life since you've been in Heaven. I know you are still always looking out for me and hope that I make you proud. I love you Grandfather!

KRIS SICHMELLER

JIMMIE LEE TRUMAN

My Granddad, Jimmie Lee Truman, was 75 years old when he left us. We'll never know the real reason why. My mother found him, passed away in his favorite chair, on January 4, 2009. I was 27 years old. He had been battling years of emphysema and COPD. I tend to think he just had enough of not being able to do all the things he used to do. He was sick with pneumonia almost exactly one year before he died and I went home to care for him. I spent a month at his bedside. I know that he thought I was taking care of him but, in reality, he was teaching me. On December 27th, 2008, Granddad called to tell me Merry Christmas. The last thing he ever said to me was, "I love you, babe." I knew, in that moment, that it was the last time I would ever talk to him. I even called my mother to tell her to go spend time with him because he would be gone within a week or so. It was the hardest phone call I ever had to make. But, the day he passed, I received the hardest phone call of my life. This letter is all of the things I want to tell him and I never got the chance to.

Dear Granddad,

This is my love letter to you. I always wake up early on the anniversary of your passing. I wonder if it will always be this way. You were and still are my hero. You were my friend, my biggest supporter, my biggest critic, my rock and my shoulder to cry on. More importantly, you were and are my Granddad. It takes a very special kind of man to live up to the name "Granddad". You were that special kind of man. You loved me unconditionally, you were there for me during some of the hardest times in my life and I am so blessed to have been there during one of the hardest times in your life. You may have thought that I was caring for and helping you, but you were actually teaching me. You taught me about compassion, love, growing older with more dignity than any person I have ever known. You showed me how to be humble and grateful. I miss those late night talks that we had when you were sick. Those nights when you couldn't breathe and we stayed up late to do your breathing treatments. After the albuterol kicked in, you would talk to me all night long. You understood and you truly cared about me. You wanted to know what I was doing with my life. You wanted to know "what I was going to be when I grew up." I am so grateful to have been able to care for you just the way you had always cared for my brothers and I. Because of you, I am in nursing school. I want nothing more for my life than to care for veterans and our American heroes. All of that is because of you.

Almost exactly one year later, you were gone. No more salty stories, no more life lessons and no more grumbling about "those damn Ritchie kids" losing your remote. Its been almost 6 years since I received the worst phone call I have ever had to endure. I didn't even believe it at first. I even called Mama a liar and that she wasn't being funny. I'm pretty sure that I just hung up on her. I couldn't accept it. It just never occurred to me that you could actually ever truly be gone. I thought you would live forever. You had always seemed so unstoppable.

All I have now are my memories and photographs. My greatest consolation is knowing that I will see you again someday. My deepest regret is that you will never see what beautiful, intelligent and funny great-grandchildren you have. Silas has those same intelligent, curious, and big blue eyes as you. Breckin is beautiful and smart. She would have probably lost your TV remote more than my brothers and I combined. She has your sense of humor and your spunk. But, I know that you would have loved them as unconditionally, fiercely and sweetly as you loved us.

If there was one lesson I learned from you, it was that grandparents have no limits on the love they have for their grandchildren.

The hardest thing I have ever had to live though was that 21 gun salute. There is such finality in the sound of those gunshots. After the final shot, it truly hit me that my hero was gone. Now, though, I know that my hero isn't really gone. You live on in the eyes of my children, in the wisdom of my aunts and uncles, in the love that my Mimi carries for you, and in the love your daughter has for my children. Those 21 shots may have felt like the end of your time on this earth but they carry a different meaning for me now. They represent your place as an American hero, not just in your love for your country but in your love for us as well. I will always miss you but I know that you are always with me. You're just a little beyond where I can see you.

Until I see you again and with all the love a granddaughter could ever have for her grandfather,

Kris

LAYNE CASE

VINCENZO "JAMES" ANGELO PITOCCHELLI & GLORIA MARIE CALANDRIELLO PITOCCHELLI

Vincenzo "James" Angelo Pitocchelli,
January 22, 1926 – January 16, 1999

Dear Daddy –

I'm writing this letter to you, sixteen years after you left us on January 16, 1999. So much happened during those last few months of your life and I never got a chance to tell you how very sorry I am that things were not good between us at that time. If you were alive today, I would be telling you how much I love you. I would ask you to forgive me and let you know I forgive you. And, I would say thank you for trying to be the best father you knew how to be.

I recently found some letters you wrote to me in 1995. The return address on the envelope said "Your Dad Always" but no address. I laugh...wondering if the mailman laughed, too, not knowing who to return it to if need be. I loved reading how excited you were we were writing back and forth. You told me over and over how proud you were of me and your granddaughters. I have such fond memories of when I was growing up. Of you playing the harmonica or powder puffing our face if we said the word "make up." My daughters remember when you would read your birthday cards, adding lots of extra words about how handsome you were, that you were the best "Nano" in the world. They would laugh and laugh, knowing you were making up the words, but loved hearing your "interpretation" of their card.

It was so hard to watch you struggle with depression. I know it wasn't easy for you. I'm so sorry for the times you felt abandoned by me. I remember trying to get help for our family, feeling so frustrated at the fact that no one seemed to want to "get involved." And, I will always feel a sense of sadness that I was not by your side when you took your last breathe like I was with Mom.

So, Daddy, I'm writing now to tell you I love you and thank you for all you did for me. You were a good and hard-working man who tried to do what was best for his family. You had a tough upbringing, little education, worked full-time in a shoe factory and part-time pumping gas. I know you loved us all very much. Take care. Please give mom a kiss for me.

PS I did take care of mom like you had asked. I hope you're proud of me.

Your daughter, Elaine

...or "Kelly Layne", the "singer" name you wanted me to use.

Gloria Marie Calandriello Pitocchelli,
November 28, 1928 – May 1, 2013

Dear Mom –

I dreaded the day your bedroom and living room in our home together would be empty. So much more I should have said. Unlike for daddy, I had plenty of time with you. It's too late to ask some of the questions I was too afraid to ask when you stopped all treatment on April 29th, 2013 like "are you sure?" I think I was in shock because I wasn't expecting you to die this time. You'd been in and out of the hospital so many times. You always rallied. This time, I visited only in the evening because I was sure you needed to rest as much as possible during the day so you could get better and come home. I was too nonchalant about this hospitalization. For that, I am so sorry. Please know I didn't let you go without asking because I didn't care anymore. You just seemed so sure. I didn't want you to see me sobbing as I did when they told us you were going to hospice.

I had to be strong for you. I had to make sure you knew I'd be okay. You even joked about how "this dying isn't like it is on TV." I didn't want to second guess you. I wanted you to have some control over your life again...although I didn't realize there would only be three days left. I knew your pain was intense. I'd been watching you suffer for eleven years and was frustrated I couldn't help you feel better.

Know how honored I was to take care of you all those years. What a blessing it was to be able to provide you with the peace and comfort of our beautiful home. I know leaving your home of 40 years in 2002 wasn't easy. You showed so much strength and courage. You endured more than most. Your sense of humor...I wish I had that. It got you through so much.

Thank you for helping me learn to be more patient, put my priorities in perspective, allowing me the privilege to be your advocate. Thank you for trusting me to take care of you. You were an amazing woman who gave much more to my family than I could have ever given you.

I miss you. I sit in your living room, now my "office" which has your pictures hanging on the wall and a beautiful hand-blown glass vase made in your honor sitting on your pedestal. You are always with me here in this space.

As you know, my girls were with me when you left this earth. We stood by and watched you go peacefully onto your next journey. We will never forget that moment.

Please give daddy a hug from me. I hope you and he are enjoying being together again, only this time with no pain for you and no depression for him. I hope the prayer shawl around your shoulders is keeping you warm and comfortable. Please show daddy my "Charlie" book and my poetry book. Hopefully, he'll enjoyed the Bible passages as well as my poems. Thanks for being my biggest fan. I could always count on you to sell a book or two everywhere you rehabbed.

I still cry sometimes when I think about you. I have to remind myself you are safe and sound, pain free, and well taken care of in the arms of God. And, I will see you both again one day.

I love you!

Your daughter, Elaine

aka "Author Layne Case"

Author/Owner
Amity Publications
www.amitypublications.com

LOGAN BETH FISHER

ILA GAUTHIER

Worth Remembering

Hello again, sweet Ging Ging. Do you have a sec? Of course...You've always had time for me.

Twenty-seven years is a long time to miss someone. There's so much I want to say Ging Ging, grandmother-extraordinaire, important words zooming and loop-de-looping around my mind like comets against a black night sky. So many things to tell you and an abundance of discoveries to share since I last saw you. Do you remember that day?

You were sleeping when I arrived. I remember the beeping and pinging of the hospital equipment that helped you stay alive. I remember your yellowed skin, your permed white-wire hair and the way you labored for air. I stood for what seemed like eons and watched your lips purse and then open--a perpetual p sound escaping on each exhale. Pwhh. Pwhh. Pwhh. And when you awakened, I remember you smiled. So like you to be happy despite pain and sadness and failing kidneys. You were my everything back then, Ging Ging, and to this day my greatest influence. And although that day was painful, I refuse to ONLY remember you that way. Instead, your memory serves as an anchor which holds me firm in the knowledge that to you I was someone special. Dear Ging Ging, remembering you makes me who I am...

My legs are squishy. My backside protrudes as does my bosom. I am a backward-shaped S. But when body image gets me down, I remember...I remember being enveloped in all of those folds, your folds, smooshed against that pillow-like chest, hug-wrapped in those jiggly arms. Instead of succumbing to society's impossible body code I smile and remember that I am built like you.

After work, there are days when I want to stomp up my porch steps, slam the front door behind me, hide away in my bedroom and stay there...maybe forever. But when gloominess takes over I remember...I remember that when you arrived for a visit to 132 Hunter Street, the backdoor would burst open and crash against the wood-paneled wall. I'd hear your high pitched "Hellooooo!' and the crackle of bags that spilled from your arms. You'd grab us joyously and plant a pink-wrinkled-lipstick-kiss directly on our mouths. I think of those kisses when I am gloomy and I sigh. Because of you, I remember the importance of being happy to see those you love.

When the "not-good-enough's" set in and the mistake-monster comes knocking at my door, when I am ready to give up, I pause, listen for your voice and I remember...I remember the stories you told me. The one about my mother sneaking out to the movies, and of my father crashing his convertible. I remember your fierce words saying, "Don't let anyone make you feel bad about yourself. Everyone makes mistakes. Everyone." I believed you then and I still do. And so when guilt and gray whisper in my ears, I remember dear Ging Ging that you loved me-- mistakes and all.

There have been moments, Ging Ging, big moments, some fear-prickled and some passionately-proud when I longed to lock eyes and hearts with you, to feel your hand on my back and hear you whisper words of support. When those "I-wish-my-grandmother-was-here" moments come, I remember...I remember the gold locket you gave me on my sixteenth birthday with the pearl inlay. I remember the envelope that you put it in and the note you wrote telling me that my grandfather gave it to you when you turned sixteen. I slip that locket around my neck and I know that you are with me. In moments of dismay and occasions of triumph, your locket is there resting on my own heart and I remember that I am not alone.

In the quiet of night, when the house is asleep and the dark invites pensivity, I sit on the side of my daughter's bed. I listen to her breathe. I watch her lips purse and open--a perpetual p sound escaping on each exhale and I remember...I remember that the kind of unconditional love that you gave to me, the kind that bolsters and sustains is the exact sort of love that I must hand down to my own children. I remember that it is my duty and honor to not only be the receiver of that kind of love, but the giver as well. My daughter, born on your birthday and baptized with your name keeps your memory close and real and I remember how to live a life worth remembering.

Logan Beth Fisher
www.muddledmother.org
www.facebook.com/amuddledmother
Twitter @muddledmother

When someone you love
becomes a memory,
the memory becomes
a treasure...

MARY CALHOUN

ELBERT CALHOUN JR.

Letter to my Brother

Dear Elbert Jr.,

Never in a million years would I have expected to lose you at such a young age. Dying of cancer was bad enough, but dying at 46 was shocking. When you were diagnosed, I promised to be there for you, do whatever you needed me to do, and push forward. It felt like a roller coaster ride. I was unable to stop time and back up. I cannot begin to understand what you must have felt, but your sister just wanted a miracle cure. You went into the hospital to surgically remove a kidney stone. You came out with a diagnosis of cancer that had already spread.

So I went with you when you flew to Houston, TX to slow down the monster inside of you. I took care of you in my home while I worked full time and also took care of our Daddy. When one of you were in the hospital, the other one was sick at home. I pushed forward and held tightly to hope.

But in time the cancer monster won. Within a week's time you lost all of your strength, fell into a coma like state and stopped breathing. It was October 28, 1994 in Dothan, AL. You were 46 and I was 33. That boisterous laugh would be no more.

No matter how hard life was for you, you never missed work, overlooked all of the bullying you faced in the public eye and kept on going. You were my rock, my example, my reminder to never let anyone bully me.

Losing you crushed my heart. It never crossed my mind that you wouldn't be there for me. I lost my brother and asked God constantly WHY you had to go. I still do. I begged Him to let me die instead. Then Daddy died two years after you. I was alone in the world at age 35.

If I had to do it all over again, stand by you, take care of you, be there to cheer you on, I'd do it in a heartbeat. I learned the precious gift of family after I lost mama, Daddy and you. For me it was too late to change anything. I had to learn this lesson the hard way, the permanent way. I had to lose you to cherish family.

Your loss still breaks my heart today. Deep heart sobs make it feel as if you died yesterday. I will never understand why you had to go, but I will cherish the time we had together. It was a precious time of miracles, the kind that make you more compassionate and loving to those who suffer loss.

I will always be your baby sister, the one who believed in you, and look forward to a day when I see you again. You are always close to my heart and my thoughts. You were my big brother, my protector, my counselor, my friend. There will never be another one like you.

Mary Jean Calhoun

Wilmore, KY

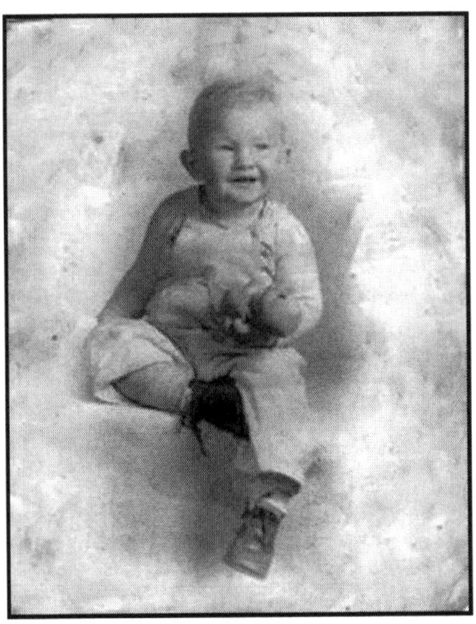

MELODY TURNER ROBINSON

DUANE TURNER

A Letter To Heaven For My Dad - Duane Turner

First Class - Airmail - Letter To Heaven, addressed to Duane Turner

Hey Dad, if I had the chance to sit on a bench & visit with you, I would...... In the meantime as I sit here, I'm writing this letter to you in hopes that you receive it up there in Heaven... I picture Heaven as being the most beautiful, peaceful place where everyone that goes there, (God heals by calling us home) is back to their healthy selves again & that we're reunited with all of our family members, friends & pets!!

I have so many questions to ask & so much to tell Ya...

1st - on the day that God took your hand to bring you to Heaven, is it everything that we were told it would be??

2nd - is there really a Rainbow Bridge that our pets cross over to wait for us & if so, was Smokey, Tarah, Ginger & DW waiting there with tails wagging to re-unite with you??

I prayed that when you got there, GramPa & GramMa Turner along with Aunt Betty, our Brother Maurice & Cousin Darren were there to meet you... I'm pretty sure that Stan's Mom & Dad, Rose & Peter were there as well...

Gosh Dad, I just want to tell Ya that the day you left us, things happened so darn fast and I'm so sorry that I never got a chance to say Good Bye or til we meet again!!

When my feet hit the floor that morning, I never dreamed that it was going to be the last day you'd be here with us!! I find that it's still hard knowing that I'll never be able to look right into your beautiful Hazel Colored Eye's again or even hear your positive words of wisdom and encouragement... I just wished that I could have stressed to you more on how much of an impact that you have made in my life & how proud I am to call you My Dad!! I Love You So Very Much!!

You were a man that if you had any "free time for yourself," it was never yours!!

You wore your heart on your sleeve & you were always helping out others... I never got to tell you just how Amazing you were & still are in my Heart!!

I want you to know that since you left us, we now have five new additions to our family tree.... You knew about Harley's first born, but weren't able to see or meet him because God needed you a couple of days before they were to come down & visit you & Mom at your home... Then they had two more little girls... Next, Katie-Jo had another little girl, & Jim finally got his little boy, so all in all, you're a Great-Granddad of eight more & that brings the total up to thirteen now. They're all so beautiful & they're growing up like weeds!!

I would like to take this time to say "Thank-You Dad" for everything you've taught me & for being there for Stan & I and the kids.

Not a day goes by that you're not in my Heart, Thoughts & Prayers.

I'm sending lots of Love & Hug's To Y'all.

I Love & Miss You Bunches -Til we meet again Dad.

Always & Forever, Your Daughter - Melody.

MIKE CASSIDY

ROSCOE CASSIDY

Dear Dad

As I set down to write this letter I realized that it is probably the first letter I have ever written to you for you were always there. Losing you was the hardest thing I have ever done next to sending my son off to Iraq. I can't honestly write this without telling you how mad I am for you leaving me, you always said "I hope you live forever and I never die" and I believed you would always be here.

Dad, I know you as a father, a supporter of my life but I had no idea of your military accomplishments until I was making your arrangements, which you never talked about. Dad you were a National Treasure to a lot of people, as the saying goes you don't know what you've got until it's gone. The National attention, International attention that you received Dad, you would have been so proud and shocked to all the attention you received. Dad, Preston will never be the same for you were a cornerstone of this community, not a day goes by that you are not mentioned at the store "Blevins Grocery". You were a friend to many, and loved by all, and missed. And I have also moved back to the home place as you asked me to do.

In my 60 of your 107 years of life there is no place I can go or nothing I can do that I don't think of you. Your love of music and dance we both shared as our whole family did. Our daily trips together, our times as we would just set and have your daily shot of moonshine.

Dad, you have taught me so much, and could have been so much more had I just listened, but as a child, teenager we seem to think we know it all, but you stood by me let me learn life's lessons and without me even knowing it guided me thru life.

I know we were not always a family who said "I Love You", but we always knew we were loved and cared for. Dad, I miss you so much for you were my inspiration to go on, you always in your own way "which was always your way" knew what to say and when to say it,. I know at your new home in heaven you are setting around with all your old friends that have gone on before you, telling those stories and whittling on those pieces of cedar as I have watched you do so many times. I know you are home now with your Mom and Dad, Mom and Mona. Please give them a big hug from me, and let them know that they are missed and loved.

Dad, don't worry about me for you have prepared me for this day, it's time for me to step up and be the man that you always knew I could be. I just hope I can be as tender as you, as tough as you, caring and giving as you.

Until we meet again Dad, I miss and love you, and to keep up your tradition will have a drink for you. And as you always say "I hope you live forever and I never die".

Love you Dad,

Your son,

Mike

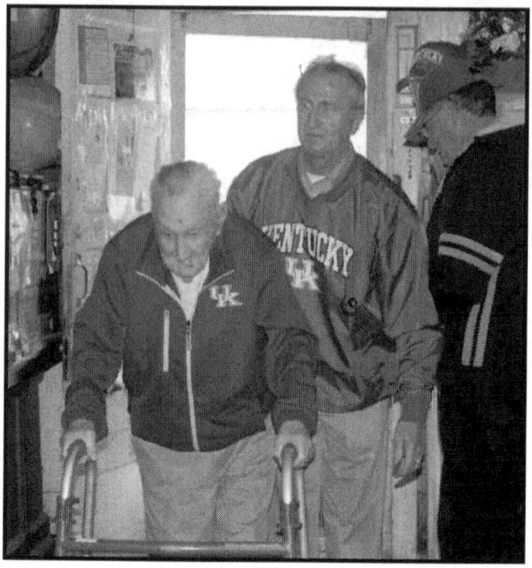
KENTUCKY
UK
UK

MISCHELLE MILLER

MEGAN MILLER

My Dearest Megan,

It's so hard to believe that it's been almost 9 years since you left me. Not a single day goes by that you are not thought of. I'm writing you this letter to tell you how my life has been going since you went to Heaven. I really never pictured my life without you, I was the one supposed to be teaching you about life and you were the one teaching me. Losing such a precious gift makes you realize how short life is. Because of you, I started a seatbelt campaign. Because of you that is saving lives. You have made me a stronger person, a person that now can reach out to other parents that have lost their child. Losing you has impacted our whole community. With this campaign I've put up billboards all over town, each month so people will see your face and maybe think that could be their child on there. Maybe take the two seconds it takes to put their seatbelt on. On March 19th 2006 you changed my life forever, I felt so lost without your smile and your laugh. I never thought I'd lose you at the age of seventeen, you were so on fire for life. You couldn't wait to graduate and have a family. I couldn't wait to see what kind of mother you would be, because you loved children. That's the part that makes me sad but I smile now, knowing you are watching over me, guiding me, leading me. In all my struggles, I go back to the day you left and seeing you laying there helpless and there was nothing I could do. I prayed that God would take you in his arms, and he did! You have changed our whole family. You have made us learn to take life one day at a time. You would be so proud of your brother and sister, they looked up to you so much. I believe you walk with them every day. I hope you are looking down from Heaven and smiling and that you are proud of the legacy we have continued in your honor. The lives you have touched are countless ways you have made known you still live. Some days it seems like yesterday you left me and others it seems like forever. What I would do to hold you again, hear your voice say I love you. I can hold onto memories and look at pictures knowing I will see you again. You have given me hope and strength, and sometimes when it's quiet I can hear you whisper, "I love you". My heart knows where you are, I will see you again someday! Megan, I love you so much, you're still my baby girl. So hard to believe you would have been twenty-seven, I have to wonder all the time what you would be doing. I know you would have been successful. You were so smart and strong willed, I look in the mirror and see you because you have made me that way. Thank you for showing me who I am, when I was the one showing you who you were supposed to be.

Forever my girl,
Your Momma
(Mischelle Miller)

Missy Covill

ROGER PRATT

If I had the chance to tell you, just how much you meant to me....

Out of all the friends I've ever had, you were the dearest and most influential.

The day I received the call, my heart sank, knowing something was wrong when the paramedics asked if I knew you. The man who was on the other end of the phone had a nervous tick to his voice and stated that the paramedics tried to revive you, with no luck. My knees were weak, and my mind just couldn't accept the fact that you were gone.

The memorial service was special, and the church was full of people who shared many stories about you. There were many stories, but most impressive, was how you were a world renowned Karate instructor, traveled the world, and very respected by many. Here I thought you were just a guy that owned a DJ business. Boy was I surprised at everything you accomplished, and I was touched by how humble you always were.

No words could ever say how much you meant to me, and how thankful I am that you came into my life. The extra mile you always went, the times I needed a friend and you were there, the times I needed to be scolded, you did with just a look, the drive to always move forward, you were the gasoline, the days when I couldn't get up and get moving, you were my will, and the heartbreak I went through, you welded it back together with reason.

All the memories we made, brings a smile to my face. The trips to Sturgis are always a great memory. The time you drove to Sturgis in a white van with a camper and ended up coming back to Michigan in a red suburban and a uhaul because you fell asleep at the wheel, flipping the camper over and all our belongings exploded on the interstate.

Throughout the years, and all the inspirational conversations and advice, I never took the time to tell you just how much I appreciated you, and how much you meant to me. You were like a grandfather to my children and a father/friend to me. I took for granted that you would always be here, and just assumed you knew. The way you believed in me like no one else ever has, and all the time you put in to making my dreams come true is something I will always hold dear. Thank you for helping to heal my broken heart, and being a very special part of my life.

Ten minutes before your funeral service I wrote a song for you, called 'Some Day'

(c). Some Day, I'll see you again, well I'll meet you at those pearly gates, with a guitar in my hand. Ya, Some Day, I'll tell you about, the way you touched my heart and soul, You changed my life and that's no doubt. Well it's killing me inside—Strength is so hard to find----But I know Some Day, you will see, that I remembered everything that you ever taught me. Some Day, we'll talk about, all the crazy dreams and the things I've seen, and how it all worked out. Well it's killing me inside—Strength is so hard to find----But I know Some Day. * In memory of Roger Pratt

Thank You

Missy Fitzpatrick Covill

www.ironcowgirl.com
Facebook / Twitter
Iron Cowgirl Missy, LLC
Iron Cowgirl Publishing, LLC

PAiSTe
PAiSTe

WCHG

NICOLETTE GARDNER

DONALD G. HABERMAN

I wrote this with know help

Dear God,

Now that you have Met grampy in person well angle, I hope that you like him because every,body else does. As you wish we will try tobe calm as this loved one has fallen into your fait. your love is like a wind that never stops flowing gracefuly, but grampy has a sun that never stops shining brightly and warmly. I know he snores pretty loudly though because he once fell asleep in my room! I know that he loves aunty bev and went serching for her right when he got to heven. He was a nice

helpful man with lots of stratagys
and happy thoats that he's willing
to share. He's stretching his wings
up there. please make sure he's happy
until we go up to see him our selfs.
Please get this message to grampy
that we love him and miss him and
repont back to me. He is in a
better place. Amen

KA **Angel's Pennies**

I found a penny today
Just laying on the ground.
But it's not just a penny
This little coin I've found.

Found pennies come from heaven
that's what my Grandpa told me.
He said Angels tossed them down
Oh, how I loved that story!

He said when an Angel misses you
They toss a penny down,
Sometimes just to cheer you up
To make a smile out of your frown.

So don't pass by that penny
When you're feeling blue.
It may be a penny from heaven
That an Angel's tossed to you. KA

PAM CREIGHTON-HAUSCHILD

HELEN CREIGHTON

Dear Mom,

It's been seven years since I held your hand as I prepared myself for life without you. I like to think that you were met by Baba and Jeje when you crossed over as I felt their presence in the room. I am forever grateful that I was with you when you took your last breath as you were with me when I took my first.

I imagine you laughing and reminiscing with family and friends that passed before you and it makes me happy to think of the stories you might all be sharing. I wish I could hear them just one more time.

I went to Europe last year and hoped to locate any living relations, but records have been lost or destroyed, and villages that you spoke of no longer exist, so success was not mine. There is no one left who can give me direction on where to look so this will have to be an ongoing project as I know they are out there somewhere and I am determined to find them.

Dad, will be 89 this year and is doing well and still living at home. He has your urn on the dresser and says he talks to you every morning. He still expects to find you at the kitchen table drawing when he gets up in the morning. I have the cards you made in a special place and when I look through them, I can sometimes feel you near me. My hands are just like yours so when I am holding the cards it is if you are the one holding them.

So many times over the years, I have come across notes and letters that you had hidden amongst my things. I think you knew how much I would love finding them after you were gone. The last letter I found was in the recipe box you had given me the last time you came to visit. Thank you for the encouraging words and most of all for the love I felt when I read it. I hope that I will find more and keep finding them for years to come. I always seem to find one just when I need it most.

I am now at an age where I think about the way it was with family near and find myself thinking of those who are no longer with me. I have so many good memories and I am so thankful that you were my Mom. You were there during my successes and failures, heartbreak and loss, laughter and joy and you always knew that tomorrow could be better than yesterday as long as I believed it would be. You allowed me to find my own way and place in the world and I will never forget your encouragement to live my life, even though it would change yours.

I am grateful:

For your unending support and love

That you taught me compassion and giving

That you taught me to stand up for what I believe in

That you taught me to be self-sufficient

That you taught me to love and forgive

That you taught me to believe and dream

And that in time, joy replaces sadness

You are always in my heart - till I see you again,

Pam

PATTIE BERTOGLIO

EDWARD F. BERTOGLIO

1/20/1925 - 11/30/2005, 80 yrs. Old

Dear Dad,

It's hard to believe it's been almost 10 years since you left your human experience for your eternal spiritual home. I thank God every day for allowing me the years I had with you as my loving father. You always took your role as a father seriously whether it was as a provider, protector, mentor and as an example of what manhood should be. You set the benchmark high when it came to my choice of boyfriends and my future husband and I thank you for giving me the confidence and self-esteem to become an independent strong woman.

After giving it much consideration I thought what one word I would use if I were asked to describe you with only one word. Generous is the word that comes to mind and describes you fittingly. When I was a child you were always generous with your time, there was never a time when I needed a playmate or Tudor to help me with my schoolwork or a taxi driver that you ever said no, no, you're too tired after a long day's work or no, not right now, I have a ballgame to watch. Even through the years you always made yourself available when needed and I just want you to know how much that meant to me!

You were also generous in spirit and lived a life of affirmation and never had a bad thing to say to anyone or about anyone. You always were able to see the best in people and people responded back to you with respect and loyalty. To this day I run into people whose life you touched and they'll share how much respect they had for you and they'll tell me, "Ed was sure a good man," Ed was the best boss they ever had," "I sure miss Ed, he always made me feel good about myself." And I'm thinking, "That's my Daddy!"

I could go on and on but in closing I want to thank you for making it a little easier when I was at your bedside when you took your last breath. I also want you to know even though you were declared brain dead after you sustained a cardiac arrest, that moment of clarity when you lifted yourself up to kiss my sister, I understand and I hold no hurt, I think you knew she needed it more than I and I'm glad she had that tender moment.

There were no words unsaid, or feelings unknown so I was able to say goodbye knowing we were always at a good place, that tender tie between a Father and a daughter that bonds us eternally. Love you, to heaven and back.... Pattie Bertoglio

REGINA PARKER & PENNY ROBBINS

JEANIE COOSE

Who Are You?
You are a lap to swing on in the backyard
You are a day at the shore
You are part of the Sunday drive to the dairy joy Tribe
You are a kiss on the top of the head
You are the supply sergeant for the tree-house warriors
You are the one gasping "He's going to kill himself on that thing" as her daredevil child flies by on his mini-bike
You are the garden keeper
Your are the Rock hunter
You are the phrase "Don't do that to your baby sister"
You are the lover of good jokes
You are the buoy trapper
You are the look of wonder as your trick cyclist child flies down the hill and straight into the woods and the crowd shouts "use your brakes"
You are always there when we need you
You are super woman
You are the judge looking down at a forged report card and the 2nd and 4th grade counterfeiters
You are the master of all games

You are a smile that outshines the sun
You are the lady who tried to convince her crying little child how beautiful she looked in her pearl white jeweled, cat eye glasses
You are a 6-foot tall sunflower from Birchcrest
You are the one who said "everyone get your coats, your baby brother really ran away this time" and was then found sleeping in the coat closet
You are the hen with your Five Baby Chicks snuggled under your wings
You are the family barber, beautician, seamstress and head chef
You are the rescuer of sleepwalking children
You are a close friend of Santa Claus
You are a bouquet of dandelions and daises in a child's up-reached hands
You are a smile when thought of
You are a lifetime full of childhood memories
You are the greatest treasure known
Who are you? ***We call you Mother –***
And the dearest Mother in the world, is the one we call our own

LOVE YOUR PARENTS
AND TREAT THEM
WITH LOVE AND CARE.
FOR YOU WILL ONLY
KNOW THEIR VALUE
WHEN YOU SEE
THEIR EMPTY CHAIR.

SHERI MEEKINS

RORIE SIMMONS JOSLIN

Addressed to: My grandangel, Rorie Joslin

Rorie gained her wings on August 3rd, 2014 – she turned 5 on July 29th and passed 5 days later.

Rorie was diagnosed with Hypodiploidy A.L.L. Leukemia on 11/20/2012. She beat the cancer but after 3 bone marrow transplants ~ her little body was exhausted from the battle.

I was 51 when she left.

My sweet Rorie!

I talk to you every day, every hour of every day but it's not the same with you being above. Having more tears than I could have ever imagined having, our "talks" bring me so much comfort. I know you are there, listening, smiling and tilting your beautiful head. I hear you saying "Oh Honey!" while batting those big blue eyes at me, it brings me smiles.

You are the strongest person I will ever know in such a tiny, little package. Your fight, strength and attitude changed my life and so many others. What an inspiration you were and still are! You endured more in your short 5 years than most can imagine – never complaining about being sick or the pains I'm sure you were having to endure – I hope you are free of them now. Still hearing you tell me "It's okay Honey, I know it's because I have Cancer" haunts me daily. Those words should have never been spoken by you, a child, you comforting us.

My heart is so broken! The pain has changed a bit but is still raw. I never thought we would have to let you go. I watched your mother give birth to you, I held you as soon as you were born, I loved you so very much, I was blessed to be with you through your journey, I held your hand as you took your last breathe. I'm so sorry I told you it was okay for you go then begged you to stay and not leave us. I know there was no way my pain and fear of losing you could have compared to your pain or fear of leaving. Every day there's little things that I remember or can still hear and see you doing, they make me smile and often laugh out loudly. They bring a great, happy laughter but still some sadness knowing we will never have those moments with you again.

There's no comfort anywhere to fill the void of you being in heaven and not here with us. It's so hard for me to understand how God needs you more than we needed you here. You had so many waiting in heaven for you, to love you and help you there but I'm sure you hit those pearly gates with your strong, loud and proud attitude. Ready to take charge of the clouds and stars!

I can only imagine how busy we've kept you, watching out for us all. I try hard not to mourn you, cry or be sad as much. It's so very hard! Mom, dad and sister need you helping them the most. You're mom has been so very strong but so very frail I believe, I can't help her and that breaks my heart more. I know you're there with her. Mackenzie is quiet a lot, she misses you so terribly. I know you and she have conversations and I pray you will always let her know you're right there with her through her life. She needs you the most to guide her. Please always send them signs and let them know you are near.

Hoping we gave you more happiness and you always know how very much we loved you, more than what anything could have brought you pain. I never thought we would lose you! I wish there would have been more times for me to have made you smile, laughed deeply, played and had done more fantastic little girl things with you, made all your dreams come true. I never thought there would be no more time for such. I cherish and miss our tea parties, hearing you sing and do your little wiggle dances, your love of funky sunglasses and all your beautiful little girl ways not to mention your love of Texas! You were and I'm sure are up there – mighty and fierce!

I literally count the days until I can see you, hug and kiss you again!

Your Honey!

Sheri Meekins, Rorie's "Honey"

Gypsy Honey's Vintage & Now Sales

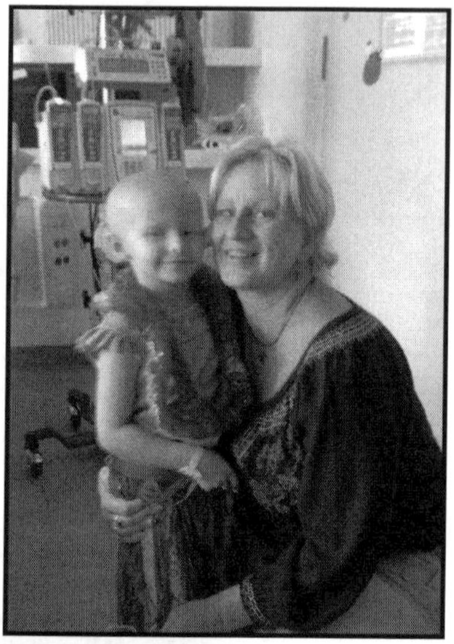

I WISH I COULD
CLIMB UP TO HEAVEN
TO GIVE YOU A HUG
AND TELL YOU
HOW MUCH
I LOVE YOU AND MISS YOU.

TERESA WINGLER ALEXANDER

ROBERT ALEXANDER

June 4, 1956—November 10, 2003

age 47 Wife, Teresa L Alexander, age 45 on his death.

January 26, 2015

Words cannot explain the hurt I feel without you next to me experiencing all the things we decided we would do as we grew old.

Each day there seems to be more leaving this life and arriving at yours. So I know you have company, I don't worry so much. I miss and love you with all my heart and always will. There is not a day that goes by that I wonder, what if I had forced you to go to the Doctor earlier, would it have given me more time with you, there is no comfort in any answer I arrive at....so I will fill you in on what our kids, and grandchildren have accomplished, always with you in close in mind.,,,

Tyson, has grown into quite a young man, you would be proud of him what he has done with the horses, I gave him your Billy Cook saddle, I know you would approve. He loves you so and misses you so, it took him several years to say your name, now there is not a day that goes by that your name is not mentioned in some fashion at the dinner table. He has a wonderful girlfriend, Josey that you would love! Her love for animals is amazing! She has a pet pig named Maple, she sits for treats!

Kirsti is graduating high school this year, accepted at Franklin College, still cheering!

Avery is 13 now, the image of Wayne.

Emry came along after you left us, she is all cowgirl, you would love her, big beautiful blue eyes, tiny, but full of spirit.

I miss you, the talks of the things we would do as we grew old, just memories now. Each day I vision us on the front porch rocking in our chairs, watching the rain, laughing at something we had done that day.

I miss the rides on the tractor we would take, singing Green Acres.

I miss the touch of your hand, the sound of your voice, you were my rock, I have had to learn to move on and trudge through this life on my own. I have made decisions, some right, some wrong, without you to lean on they seems so hard.

I kept the farm, even without insurance, I made a promise to myself that I would for the grandkids, which is what we decided a long time ago we would leave to them. I work a lot of hours but I am making it! I have a great job now, very good people.

I feel like giving up, but I know you would not have it that way, so I am dealing with life the best way I can without you. You were my rock, my sanity, sometimes I feel I can't go on, but I hear you say "stop it, it's not your time"!

At the end of the day, I reflect on the everyday happenings that go on, the what ifs and the could have been, but in the end its still the same each day, without your good night kiss I drift off to sleep and if I'm lucky I dream about you, it seems so real, I feel like you talk to me in my dreams, so in closing until the day we are reunited, I want you to know that I love you and always will, and one day we will be together again my love. Until that day I go on, but I know when the time comes, you will be there with your arms open for me once again

Love You Always, Teresa

I LOOK TO THE SKY AND TALK TO YOU.
WHAT I WOULDN'T GIVE TO HEAR YOU TALK BACK. I MISS YOUR VOICE, I MISS YOUR LAUGHTER. I MISS EVERYTHING ABOUT YOU.

TERRY PLAISTED

CASIMIR THADDEUS ZWARYCK

Died Oct. 7, 2013 – 97 years old, Age related cardiac arrest
I was 7 days shy of my 62nd birthday on Oct. 15th

Dear Daddy,

They say when cardinals are around us; it means that our loved ones who have passed are near!

I have, for as long as I can remember, seen cardinals in the yard, at the feeders and in the trees. I never thought about how often I see them until just recently. From the day you left this earth, I have sensed you close by; and I often find myself saying, "Dad, can you believe this?" The same with Mom; and I am so happy that you two are once again together after so many years….watching all of us as our lives continue to play out.

The memories, the pictures emblazoned in my heart and mind are priceless. Often, when I do or say something, I think about how did I know how to do that or how did I know what to say just at the right time? I know it is your (meaning you and Mom) influence in my life…the things I saw you do or heard you say. I can hear it plain as day, "Terry, you can do anything you put your mind to."

I think one of the most important things I learned from you both was, no matter what the situation, "Always, do the right thing". I pray that I have passed along that wisdom to my children, grandchildren, and others.

Now that you are in Heaven, I hope you can look back with no regrets about your life. I have always been very proud of you as you always worked so hard to provide for us. We all depended on you to come through for us and everyone else who knew you depended on you too. If there was anything that needed fixing, it would be brought to you to fix. If there was anything that needed to be built, you could do it…way back to the snow forts in Greenlawn when I was a kid. And, you always made everything an adventure, even a trip to the dump……

One adventure to the next was how you lived your life. I so enjoyed the three years that you were with us in Georgia where your sense of adventure continued...what an imagination at age 90 something!! Seeing you almost every day was a gift from God; and I cherish the opportunity to have shared so much one on one time with you then. It helped me identify your strengths in me; and your weaknesses too. As you always said, "no one is perfect". Now I can say, "It's the balance of strengths and weaknesses that's important!" You were perfect the way you were, and me as I am.

I remember sending a card to Mom in Florida during whatever family drama was occurring at the time; and inside that card was a little piece of paper on which I wrote "Mom, Don't ever lose your sense of humor!" She taped it to her mirror in your bedroom. Almost twenty years later, you gave me that piece of paper when we were living in Georgia; and I could not believe you still had it. I was so happy! It told me that I had shared some of my wisdom with you. It is a treasure now for me.

So many little keepsakes, quotes, sayings over the years…..

I hope you are proud me!

Until we meet again, I love you, I miss you, I think of you every day!

As you always ended our conversations in person or on the phone, "Keep in touch, we love you!!!!"

Forever, your loving daughter,

Terry Zwaryck Plaisted

Mom
Don't ever

TIM BURTON

MIKE PELLETIER

Dear Uncle Mike,

It's so hard to believe that you have been gone so long that I can't even remember the date you left. I remember visiting you the night before in the hospital, and so many times before that. I remember asking myself why my mother and you had to be together, and why you both had to leave us here alone. On May 8th 1976, when I was only 15, I remember seeing you through the window of the camper that I was watching your daughter in. You brought it to the hospital so you could stay with us and your sister in Buffalo to help and support us. I'll never forget seeing you carrying my mother's pocketbook and coat across the parking lot knowing then what you were about to tell me.

You used to do the books for your gas station in that pick-up truck camper parked in your driveway at home, so you could concentrate on your work without the distractions of us, and your two wonderful daughters. I remember coming in there and bothering you, though to you, it was just another small interruption. You would explain what you were doing, and then I'd get the hint and leave you alone to go about your work. It seems you were always in your flannel shirt, blue work coat and blue work pants.

You used to let me pump gas at your gas station in South Glens Falls (Mike's Sunoco), and every now and then, to the dismay of my mom, that you so kindly took into your home and cared for until her dying days, you would give me a couple bucks, and I felt rich. I often rode my bicycle 15 miles one way to spend time there with you.

Well Uncle Mike.....I still feel rich... because I knew you. You taught me so many things that no one else ever did. You taught me to be kind, thoughtful, respectful, genuine, loving, caring, and the list goes on. You taught me how to change tires, change oil and be honest. I had a 31 year career in the transportation business and raised two incredible children, because I knew you. I started at that job, as I did with you, pumping fuel. I listened and learned and grew to be one of the best in my field. Again, without you, I am not sure any of this would have happened.

I only took my wife to my mother's grave site once, and that was the day we buried you. I have not been back to either. I hope that is OK with you. I don't feel anything there except sorrow and pain. When I reflect in this vain, I feel so much more. A friend of a friend suggested I write a letter to heaven, and the tears I am shedding, and the pride I am feeling as I do this are a healing that I think I have needed for years.

I never got a chance to tell you what you really meant to me, and what a mentor and hero you were. You know all too well that my father abandoned us when I was around two years old. You knew more about my family than I ever did, or ever will. Losing my Mom was hard, then losing you, your sister (my Aunt) Carole, and finally Aunt Joan. All four of you to cancer at 38, 45,48 and Aunt Joan was lucky to reach her 70's. She would not let anyone tell me until she was gone, which hurt more than knowing I think. I was going into the hospital for a defibrillator implant, so I could not even go to her wake or funeral. I was quite hurt by that because we had been in contact many times over the years. She was worried about my heart and did not want to burden me I guess.

I am now on my fourth defibrillator, so thankful that # 3 did its job, my wife of 30 years is also still in the Medical Field as a Certified Medical Assistant and our daughter has gone on to be a Clinical Laboratory Scientist. Our wonderful son Cory is a High School English Teacher, Baseball, and Golf coach. He's getting married soon to a wonderful woman named Shannon Rossi, and you would be so proud, as are we.

I always say that I hope to understand someday why things happen the way they do.

Maybe you and Little Mike have the answers.

Thank You from the bottom of my heart for all you did for us.

I Love You.

I never had the chance to say that to you and for that I am truly sorry. I hope we meet again someday, although I must be honest and say I hope 30 years from now is OK with you.

Your nephew, Tim Burton (with wife Laurie)

TINA DONBECK

ROBERT DONBECK

Age 28 when he passed in a car accident; I was 8 years old.

To the Father I Wish I Knew,

I don't have many memories of you. Over the years I've tried hard to conjure up images of you in my head but only a few appear. I can remember the odd clicking sound you would make when clearing your throat, almost like a nervous tick. I recall your red plaid button down shirt that you would wear often with a crisp white t-shirt underneath. I remember your awkward tallness, your hush puppy brown eyes, like mine and to this day on the rare occasion when I catch a whiff of English Leather it reminds me of the few times you carried me and my little nose would nestle in your neck. Those are likely simple memories to many but those are all that I have and I cherish every one.

I was 8 years old when you passed. November 4, 1981. I remember that day quite vividly. I recall getting ready for school only to have my morning routine interrupted by a knock at the front door of the house that my Mother now shared with her new husband. It was the local police. I didn't think too much about their presence; my stepfather was the town's Fire Chief, men in uniform were not an uncommon sight at our house. I recall my Mother standing at the door looking back at me with a worried look on her face and then she quickly ushered me out to the school bus. The day was seemingly like any other day to me and it would take years to completely understand the implication of events that had occurred; it wasn't until I got home from school and saw my Grandmother and Mother sitting on the couch weeping, did I get a hint that something in my world was about to forever change. I recall my Mother's face as she said the words "Your father died this morning." I looked at her eyes, swollen with black stains from a mixture of her mascara and hours of tears. I knew that I should be crying too but the tears did not come; it took some time for the tears to finally arrive and years since to completely understand everything I had lost that day.

When you are 8 years old you do not understand the significance of loss that comes with death. You haven't experienced enough of life yet to understand that something is and will be forever missing. As I grew up and matured, as milestones and achievements came and went, I understood more about what it meant to lose a Father. I lost a piece of my heart and identity. Even today, 34 years later, I search to understand the elements of me that are you. Do I get my witty sarcasm from you? Do we have the same sense of humor? Did you have a restless spirit like I do? Were you creative? Moody? What made you happy at the start of each day? Did you love passionately and did you forgive quickly? Did you like sunrises like I do? When I watch my two boys growing up, I can't help but wonder how much of you are in them. And I can't help but wonder if you brought them to me to help me better understand myself?

My oldest son Aidan, was born November 4, 2008. He arrived over a week early, which is very rare for a first child. Throughout that pregnancy I thought of you often, more so than usual...it saddened me to know that your first Grandchild would be born without you ever knowing or holding him and even more aware that he would never know you. To this day I truly feel you were present with me as I gave birth to him. It feels odd to say I could feel you around me, but I did. I like to think you sent him (both my boys) to me on that day, that most horrible day where I used to think about nothing more than the hole that was left in my life when you left...and now that day is filled with such joy and happiness and you. And even if I never know the answers to all my questions about whom you were at least not in this life; I like to think I'm learning more about you by watching both of my boys grow into men. Perhaps they are showing me who you were and who you could have become.

With that, I thank you for being my Father, for giving me this wonderful life. I sincerely hope we meet again in whatever comes after...until then, I love you Dad, whoever you were you are everything to me.

Tina

Tina Donbeck

CAROLINE BAROT

Died February 2, 2012; she was 56 I was 39

Dear Mom,

It's been a little over 3 years since you've passed away. I miss you more than words could ever express. There is so much I wish we had talked about when you were alive and so much I wish we had shared with each other. I blame myself for how our relationship ended, fractured and distant.

I spent most of my life trying to be everything opposite of who you were or at least who I thought you were. I let so much of my own anger toward you get in the way of truly understanding you; at least until your death. Your death for some reason has been a catalyst for me to begin understanding you in ways I never had. Fundamentally, I've realized that you wanted in your life what we all want…to be loved unconditionally, to feel safe and content in our own skin. How we all achieve those things is intimately our own path and I recognize yours was not always a smooth one.

For years I blamed you for not being the Mother I needed and wanted you to be…I struggled to reconcile that we would never have that Mother/Daughter relationship I had seen in the movies or seen in my friend's families. That struggle unfortunately kept us even further apart. I wanted you to be this "thing" in my life that you simply did not know how to be. What I failed to realize then is that you were the best Mother to me that you knew how to be. I know this now and I should have accepted all that you were capable to give.

Now, being a Mother myself I understand more that there is no rulebook or handbook in being a good parent. You simply do the best you can and hope that that is enough. I honestly feel you tried to be the best Mom you could. I know your own life got in to the way at times. I know having me at 17 robbed you of a youth and of experiences that you desperately wanted to have and as such I always felt responsible for much of your sadness. I want you to know that I would have done anything in this lifetime to have seen you happy…truly happy. Not the kind of happiness you painted on with different men, or fancy clothes or new "things"…but real happiness that's lasting and makes you smile from within. You deserved that.

Despite our differences and distance through the years…I loved you with all my heart. You were the one persons attention I wanted the most and you were the one I wanted to make most proud. I wanted nothing more than to protect you from the hurt I know you felt and I desperately wanted you to see that like a lotus flower, beautiful things can emerge from the mud. You were beautiful, Mom.

It is my hope that in whatever comes after this life, in to the next that you have found the peace and happiness that escaped you here and I hope that you have taken with you the knowing that you were loved unconditionally by me.

Love always.

Your daughter,

Tina

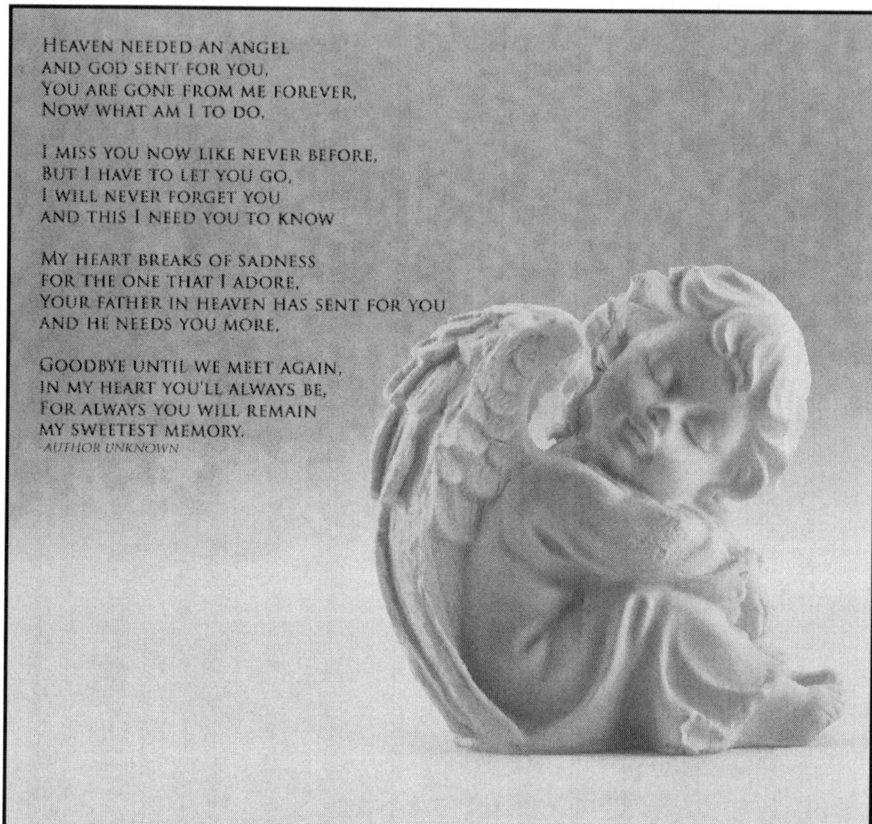
Heaven needed an angel
and God sent for you,
You are gone from me forever,
Now what am I to do,

I miss you now like never before,
But I have to let you go,
I will never forget you
and this I need you to know

My heart breaks of sadness
for the one that I adore,
Your Father in heaven has sent for you
and He needs you more,

Goodbye until we meet again,
In my heart you'll always be,
For always you will remain
my sweetest memory.
-Author Unknown

TRACY SMITH

BUFORD WAYNE WHITLEY "BITS"

To My Dear Sweet Loving Daddy

I know that the last words I said to you were "I love you". I know that you knew that I loved you, and I know that you always loved me too. I sure do miss you. I knew that I loved you, but I didn't realize just how deep that love went until now. You know that there is a piece of my soul that seems to be missing that was attached to you. It feels like a band that pulls on my soul that is connected to you. Sort of like an umbilical cord that is still attached to you even though you are there in heaven. Maybe that is a good thing, but for the last month and a half, since you were sick and passed away, I am so weak and feel as though I am faint in my soul. Maybe the umbilical cord feeling will turn out to be the way you feed me from heaven. I need strength now, whatever milk you can send my way. You always kept me safe and warm as a baby in it's mother's womb, so it makes sense that I am still so connected to you. Not just spiritually, but physically also. I know that there is no sadness there in heaven, but I know how sad it would make you if you knew how sad I was to have lost you from this world. I know that because I remember how sweet you were when you saw how sad I was over losing my dog just a couple of weeks before you got sick. I'll never forget your sweet heart and how you said that you hated to see me so sad right here at Christmas time. Right now, just knowing that if there was sadness there in heaven and you could feel my pain over losing you, not wanting YOU to be sad because of my sadness is why I am trying to overcome MY sadness. For you. I know if hearts could break in heaven, yours would break to see me so broken. So day by day, I am trying to focus on the good things here on earth. I know that I still have a lot of blessings to be thankful for in this world.

I do have a bone to pick with you! Do you remember after you had that heart attack over 20 years ago what I told you? I told you that I wanted to have my Daddy for at least for as long as you had yours, and you had yours for 94 years! So you cheated me out of sixteen years! I joke with you because I know you liked to laugh. The sad part for me though is, if I live to be the ripe old age of 94, then that means it will be another 42 years before I get to see you and feel your loving arms around me again. That's pretty much my current life over again minus 10 years. It will be so hard without you in my life physically. However, I know that 42 years is nothing compared to eternity with you and my Lord Jesus Christ. I also know that somehow, you are with me now.

I just want to thank you for all you did for me throughout my lifetime. You were truly a real "Daddy". I am blessed to have had you in my life. I am aware that some people have never been able to make that claim. So again, thank you Daddy for being MY DEAR SWEET LOVING DADDY!

From the Bottom of My Heart and Soul,

Your Daughter,
Tracy W. Smith

TRUDY HANCOCK WILLIS

FREDERICK RAYMOND HANCOCK II

Dearest Dad,

You know I never gave it any thought that I didn't have all the time in the world to be with you, but I now know that all the time in the world is just an illusion; still so much to say, to ask, to do; so much love held deep inside until we are together again.

Do you know just how much I miss you in my life? I want you to know my husband David, you'd love him dad; he is fantastic and he loves me unconditionally; believe that? Unconditionally: something I longed for from you. I know you loved me dad but why did you leave me? Not just the fact that you and mom divorced but when you left I was 3 years old. Are you aware of how I stood at that window on Smith Avenue every day waiting for you to come home? Remember you teaching me to do the twist in the living room there? I was so cheated, a family with mommy and daddy and I was cheated out of that "daughter/father relationship" I never did; Dad.

Do you know how Grant hated me? Dad, Do you know the things that I had to deal with when I was a little girl? I miss you dad, I love you so much. There are times I watch a movie, see a commercial on the "idiot box" you were so famous for calling the television set or hear a song and memories...tears would stroll down my face. I was 3 years old dad, I needed you, and Martha was so mean to me; why did you let her be so mean to us, me especially? There was so much I did not understand; why didn't you live with me anymore, did you stop loving me? I wait and wait at the window and you never come home, and then we were living in another house; can you find me? I was 5. Then when you did visit I wanted to be with you so badly but I was scared that I would do something and you would leave again; I didn't understand why you left me. Then came the long awaited long Grey Hound Bus ride to Nashville where you would be waiting, growing up seeing you only 2 weeks a year was not a father/daughter relationship make; why did you leave me dad? I wish I could visit you in heaven; I'd be there every day, there are things I want answer's to. When I was 19 years old I was pregnant and you lectured me on how I ruined my life. You asked mom for all the other kids; why didn't you ask for me? Did you not love me enough to have me live with you? Or did Martha say no? Do you know how different my life would have been if I had had an active father growing up? I am however convinced I would still have ended up with David; I am convinced God brought David and I together. Of course I would not have traded my boys; your grandchildren for ANYTHING. Dad; Do you know that I sing? I was invited to sign at Carnegie Hall. Dad; Do you know that I have a published poem: "A Baby's Cry" in a book of poems called "The Muse". I made mistakes that can't be changed but Dad; Do you realize what I went through to get my college degree. Did you see that I did it all alone with 2 sons and working 2 jobs? It meant the world to me that you were at my college graduation; I have so often asked myself, what do you think of me? You said to me that night that you are proud of me; that's all I ever wanted to hear from you and or that you maybe even thought I was beautiful, do you dad? Do you think I'm beautiful? Don’t ALL fathers think that their daughters are beautiful?

If I could have just one more day with you. Dad; Do you? Who am I dad? Am I you?, am I my grandmother, my love for flea markets and antiques I know I get from you, your mother? Who am I suppose to be "just Like"? I am not like my mother; I am honest and blunt to a fault. Are you proud of me dad? My heart aches for you daily dad, I miss not getting the opportunity to learn who each other were and you left me again; only this time you aren't coming back; I love you dad, I miss you so no words can describe.

Dad, Do you know all of your great grandchildren? They are wonderful kids and you have another on the way, Mike's. I'll never forget how it felt to hand to you your first great grandson William Michael Lee Jones; you know he is 13 years old now 13...Alex is 4 and there's Aubrey but we don't know each other well; she is 19 and was kept from us until she was 15...the next one is due 2 days before your birthday...soon.

I want to apologize for being so selfish. I stood at your bedside and begged you not to leave me again, begging you not to die and leave me again; the Doctors said that even though you could not respond; you still could hear us, tell me why is it if the heart organ itself does not actually feel pain then why does mine feels as if it has been shattered all over again. I'm sorry I was selfish; I didn't want you to go yet, if Heaven had visitation I'd always be there. At least now you are no longer suffering in pain and not being able to breath, did you know I quit smoking 7 years ago; watching you suffer and my grandson asked me to quit; said he wanted me around to meet his family. All my life all I ever wanted was for you to love me; that early morning when your children were called to your bed, one of the last coherent words you spoke were to me " I Love You" is what you said to me and my heart shatters I'll never forget that moment in my life. I once read an article about how loved ones return to you in forms of butterflies and cardinals, that they appear to you when you are sad or are missing your loved one; well I am always seeing beautiful Red Cardinals; I get solace in thinking the beautiful cardinals I see are you coming to say hello.

So time has come and gone, I'll be seeing you dad; when my day comes to join you in heaven along with my grandparents, sibling (s) aunts and uncles as well as my own unborn child who went to heaven in 1974. It will be your face I will be searching for daddy. So I'll be seeing you,,,<3

I so love you,

Trudy

TYSON SCHMIDT

TAWNEY STAR SCHMIDT

Drowned July 31st, 1998, Age 4, I was 29

My Sweet Tawney Star;

You taught me more in your 4 short years of life than any other person could the rest of my life. From you I learned how to be a much better father, how family was more important than anything else, how to give, have faith in God, how there was more important things than work and money.

I was sorry I could not be there to watch you graduate, teach you that you too deserve a man who would cherish you for you, open your doors, walk you down the aisle to be with that special man, see those great recitals, and watch you grow and learn, protect you after that first broken heart, intimidate all your boyfriends so they know how special you are, and in general spoil daddy's little girl.

I was always sorry I chose to work more and family took a back seat to the dollar. I now know that all you and any kid wants is a Mom and Dad at your side. But because of you I learned the importance of those close and to cherish every moment as you never know when someone would move on to be with the Lord.

I learned how to be a father and how to be there for my children as they grow, attend all their special occasions, and cherish those special moments to insure I would always be there for them.

You also taught me how to give with your seeing things in a better way. Your pretty blue eyes were able to provide 2 other children the gift of sight. So now they may see their way clear to lead others with this special gift that you provided them.

Things like having faith in God were a little harder to handle and took more time. Making the decision to pull you out of man's hands with the machines that kept you alive and allowing God to take on that stress was definitely the hardest decision any parent should never have to make. God was quick and fast to deliver you to his arms. He knew you were a special girl and needed to be with him. While for me the first couple years made it hard to see how a good and just God could ever take such a sweet young girl at such an early age.

Your passing has strengthened me, the Lord knew that we could handle such a tragedy and how that would strengthen us as a family once we got through the heartache, tears, and sorrow.

Learning how to forgive at this time of sorrow was one of the hardest lessons to learn. Sometimes allowing for your heart to forgive others isn't always easy when you have so much pain but with your help I was able to handle everything and forgive those who needed my forgiveness.

God gave us the greatest gift we could have asked for and we had you for 4 years to treasure. We look forward to walking with you in eternity so you can meet the rest of your family, 2 more brothers and 2 more sisters please take care of and protect all 5 of your brothers and sisters. Lord knows they need a guardian angel to protect them from all the dangers and I trust you have been there through everything. I'm sure you were standing over them as your brothers each got hit by cars while riding bikes, or when overseas in Afghanistan your there to protect them.

To help me get over the heartache of losing you your heart is alive and beating well in another person. Your passing quickly was able to help another person with that sweet heart of yours. From early on you were always sharing that huge heart of yours rather it is to smack your "best friend"/brother with a large stick or forgive him for hitting you with a shovel, or giving anything and everything you had to others without hesitation. How great it is to know that sweet heart is living on in another person.

So as I walk the streets and I look into another person's eyes I can't help but to wonder are you looking back, is there something familiar in those big blue eyes. I see someone who's sweet and loves ice skating as much as you did, is it your heart that makes them so generous. Then I realize every time I look in the mirror I see you and the little things you did to make me who I am looking back at me and thank you for that gift.

I'll always love and cherish you my sweet Tawney Star,

Love Daddy

Gods little angel,
bright shining Star, passing through our lives like a comet
Bright pink blazing by, blue eyes laughing, lips smiling brightly
Skate through the sky, as on smooth blue ice
Twirling, swirling, pink dress of ruffles
Her loving and joyful ways with us will always stay
Your families loving joy, and Gods twinkling little Star

Tyson Schmidt
Journey of Lights
http://www.journeyoflights.com
http://www.facebook.com/journeylights

ULLA TIBBETTS

URSULA PREUSS

To my mother, mutti Ursula

On a cool and rainy spring day I received I phone call from my brother, Peter from Berlin Germany.....

I guess I wasn't prepared of what I was going to endure with this phone call.

It was May14th on Mother's Day the year of 2000...

I learned that my mother had passed during the morning hours in a hospital in Berlin Germany, from complication of colon disease. My mom was born August 9, 1917 in Berlin Germany, she was 83 years old...

I just had my 55 birthday in March...

After I received this very difficult phone call, my legs just folded out from under me with disbelief....I couldn't even begin what our lives were going to be like from that day forward... There have been so many times I was thinking of sending you, my dear Mutti (mom) A letter to Heaven... So today is the day I am writing you this letter to heaven. I sure hope you will get it and share it with the Angels that are all around you....

Every birthday and holiday, mom, our family, myself, your grandchildren get balloons and before dark we send them to you....everyone gets in a circle and holds hands, and we let them go...

When I think back of my years growing up, I have so many questions for you that I felt you could never answer for me. For instance, I was about 17 and I found a birth certificate with a name of Peter Haller... And a certificate of an adoption that said Kurt Brueckmann adopted Ulla Preuss as his child..

For all these years I had no idea who that was, mom. Why could you not tell me why I was adopted and also that I had a half-brother named Peter and where he was for 19 years....

I know now your life was very secretive and all you went through, you must have been scared to tell anyone what you had endured doing your younger years.... Why did your father, my grandfather, tell you that you needed to leave home and get married to a man he picked out for you, and World War II was just around the corner. You must have been so frightened, being alone after that man you married was drafted into the war and wouldn't return, but 7 years later to find out you had given birth to a baby girl named Ulla... My nick name was Ulla putz my grandmother told me.

So many questions I have for you... How did you survive the War with no job and pregnant and having to run at all hours of the night and day to the bunkers to take refuge from the bombs that where falling on your town? And after I was born on March 10th, it was still wartime, how did you manage your fear.... I can't even imagine what and how I would handle such horrific times in history.. You where such an amazing young woman with such strength and determination to pull through these bad times....

My grandmother Hertha, your mom, passed when I was just five years old, sadly she took her life after your dad passed of kidney failure at a young age. Again I wondered how you would pull through that, so many hard times for you, mom!

Later in our lives things finally turned out better for you, I was so glad when you found my stepdad, mom ,who adopted me and gave us a better life....I am so grateful to you and my stepfather, Kurt.....

Life has been a roller coaster for me, many ups and down, mutti (mom) since you left us.

I wish you could see your grandchildren all grown up, living life and handling each and every crisis in a way that is amazing to me. I guess we all have inherited your strength and wisdom, my sweet mom.... Chris is a business woman, Kim has a great job as a coder for a health insurance company, and Brian became a Special Ed Teacher. He also published his first novel...Dream Brother..... I am so proud of all 3.. Brett is your great grandson, who you didn't get to meet...he is very businesslike, mom, like you were and very good with people, he works and also goes to a college in California. I always talked about you to him, how I learned so many things from you...even how you said I couldn't boil water ...well I didn't do too bad in the cooking department, over all, you would be pleased......

My Life Lesson from you being my mom (mutti) is, never say: I can't or it won't work... Because that wasn't allowed in your vocabulary...

I always said to my kids or myself, what would my mom have done or how would it be better if I could ask her...

You taught me to make things out of nothing, I sew all of your granddaughters clothes and they look good, mom, to my surprise..

It's really strange for me, thinking back at all your adversity, how many times I used your thinking as an example, like not being scared to move to the USA as such a young woman with a 6 week old baby girl in tow not knowing what my future would bring.....

I know you were brave letting me go, I am sure against your better judgment.

Mom, you can rest in peace, I made it. I know your smiling now and you're proud of me...

I am proud to have had you for my mom, (mutti) I couldn't have had a better teacher in my life.

You managed to live inside me every day, and there isn't a day when something will happen that reminds me of you. You are in my prayers daily, I know wherever you are, you are safe and surrounded by beauty and as I turn 70 years old or young, I am going to party with you in my heart....

I am glad I had a chance to write you this letter, my sweet Mutti, I know we will be together again and that's why I am not too afraid to join you one day...it's not my time yet. I hope I still have things to do and hopefully will be able to make peace with my son, and get to meet my grandchildren before I come and join you, mom.... I love you forever, your daughter, Ulla, or Ulla putz as you liked to call me.... Aufwiedersehn...

So with that being said, your grandson wrote you a poem on the day you passed, I want you to read it...

Omi, my grandmother...
Who escaped from East Berlin
During construction of the Wall
Running towards a new life...
A new beginning
And, at her Life's end,
She silently danced into the next,
Tracing the same steps that we all eventually take.
In search of a new Partner,
In some other time.
And in some other place.
May14. 2000

WANDA KEZAR

DORIS ADALAIDE NICHOLS

Memories of Nana

Long, black hair
With ageless wisps of white,
Dancing, brown eyes Sparkling in the light.

Face careworn,
Face of hope,
Every crease
A story to tell.

Line of sorrow,
Line of care,
Line of love,
Life to share.

Arms for want
of better days,
Open wide,
Warm embrace.

Mouth, pursed tight,
Mouth, open wide,
Laughter, wisdom
Deep inside.

Memories,
Images past,
One life, freely given,
Eternal link to past.

Doris Adalaide Nichols
1910-1992
Streets of Gold, Heaven 77777

January 15, 2015

Dear Nana,

This is the poem I wrote for you shortly after you passed away in 1992 at the age of 81. When I read it, you appear before me, so real that I could hug you and hold you one last time—that one last time that I never got to say good-bye.

You were always there for me, my precious Nana. Despite your failing heart caused by rheumatic fever as a child, you were always strong. Even from your bed, you were my father, my mother, my protector, my conscience, and my friend—my best friend.

You didn't have much, and you suffered greatly. Only later did I understand your sacrifice for me. I need you to know how much I understand it now, and I want to thank you for pointing me to true grace and forgiveness.

You knew that the only way I would survive and lead a better life was to find the Author of Life. You knew that true peace and forgiveness comes only through Christ, and you did all you could to make sure I found Him.

All those times we were left alone, not knowing what lay ahead, you held onto hope. You prayed through the pain for over fifty years, and you taught me to hope and persevere.

I still remember how much you loved the beauty of a single flower and all of the hours we spent in your flower garden watching the birds flutter about the blooms. I remember how much you loved the melodious song of the chickadee, especially in the spring after a long harsh winter. These were our simple joys, and I treasure every childhood moment we spent together.

As time went on, I grew, and I thought I needed you less. I didn't see, then, that you needed me more. I still remember (and still have) the beautiful puppy Valentine you sent me in college that simply said, "I need you, now."

I came home, but not nearly enough. After college, love and then marriage and my teaching career consumed me. I knew you understood deep down, and that you were happy for me, but you were also scared—scared that my life would turn out like yours. You were almost never wrong, Nana, but you'll be happy to know that this time you were.

You were the one who sent me to church and surrounded me as much as possible with people who taught me what real love and marriage should be. You prayed for me, and God sent me the best friend and husband a woman could have. You would be so happy and proud of your son-in-law, the pastor; your granddaughter, the writer, teacher, and mother; and your two great-grandchildren, who laugh and play and love the Lord. We are not perfect, and we fall every day, but we love God and each other deeply. Your heart would leap with joy that the circle of darkness—of alcohol and betrayal, of anger and unforgivingness that you lived has been broken by His light and love.

I have one more secret feeling—one hidden for what feels like eons of time. Really, it is the reason for this letter to you. On that spring day when your spirit needed to find its final resting place, I didn't mean to be late. We had it all planned—you and me and Psalm 23. I had it memorized since I was a child, and I reviewed it every year, but for some reason, it just wasn't meant to be, and I am sorry.

I kept asking why for the longest time, and the answer was always the same—never de-lay, never delay. Life comes and goes in a moment, and you must always be ready to share what's in your heart—to love and to appreciate, in the here and now. Always seize the day.

Don't worry, Nana. Although this was my hardest moment and my biggest regret, I know that regret is a terrible place to live. I was 24 then and only beginning to understand. I know I've been forgiven, and I'm further down this road, but I still have to be reminded of this life les-son. Maybe that's why I had to write this letter to you and why I had to tell you what you always told me. It'll all be okay because all that matters is that someday it will be—you and me and Psalm 23.

Love forever,

Wanda

YVONNE PRINCE

JANET LOGAN

Dear Grandmother Janet Logan,

Tho you have been gone since 1805, I wanted to let you know how much I love you. While there are no photos, I know what you would look like. All of the Logans are dark haired, rather short, rugged, and they smile alot. The women are beautiful and the men handsome. I would recognize you!!

I know you fell in love with, and married, a Presbyterian from Scotland. Beyond being frowned upon, being Methodist Irish, this marriage caused you, your husband, and children to be disowned by both families.

Whilst he was "only fit" to be a garbage man (grave digger was an honor and he was a disgrace), you were able to stay home with the children. I don't know why he died at 42 (buried in the woods, at night, with no marker and no service), but being widowed with five young children was a death sentence. I cannot imagine my children starving to death, yet they would have back then. With no social services and only family and church, (both turned their backs to you), all of you would have died. I understand that if you begged, you would have been arrested!

I am so proud that you took the offer of free passage to Nova Scotia for you and the children in 1761! How scary the trip on the "coffin" ship must have been. Did everyone recover well? How exciting to arrive in Nova Scotia and become one of the first women to be granted land in Truro! I'm sure it was a hard life, but it was your life. What a sigh of relief, and pride, you must have felt. Today Logan Street, Truro, has very expensive properties on it. When folks think "Logan" and equate it to your street, they think success. You were a success in the 1700's and that continues.

When I go to Ireland, everyone wants a copy of your Port of Entry papers to Nova Scotia. Your papers were 40 years before the official records, outside of local churches. Now you are an unsung heroine for standing up for you and your children! Now there is a Presbyterian/Methodist Church in Ireland. I've heard stories of your hardships in Ireland and I've heard stories of what you faced in Nova Scotia. I know, you fought, worked hard, loved, and rose above it all and provided for your family in an amazing manner.

We know your amazing DNA is alive and well in the Logans of today. Your legacy is of honest, hardworking, people and like you, their families are their life. The Logan women can be feisty, strong willed, but with huge hearts. You even have a descendant who has an airport named after him! I am so proud to be an ancestral granddaughter of yours. Being a single mother, when I had troubled times, I used to think about what you went through and then realize how blessed I was. Life is different in the 21st century, but in many ways it has stayed the same. Whether single or not, all mothers do the best they can for their children.

I have so many questions for you. What was a day in your life in Ireland and, later, in Nova Scotia really like? Logans loved to dance, did you dance in Truro, perhaps at a barn raising? What was my ancestral grandfather like? What was your maiden name? Being an outcast, even the church records were stricken of that and your existence. Did you fall in love again? Did you go to church? Alot of people left Ireland for religious reasons. Did you help create a new, accepting, church? I do know, the Logans were, and are, God loving people and non-drinkers. That hasn't changed much either!

Grandmother, I'm sure all of the Logans that have gone, and will go, before me have asked you many questions. However, I plan on my time on the bench, in Heaven, with you. Perhaps, I'll have a question or two that hasn't been asked.

Till we meet on the bench,

Love,
Yvonne Logan Chaffee Prince

From Eileen

It has been quite a journey publishing Dedications-Dads & Daughters, and Keepsakes, Treasures From the Heart in April 2013. Most people will deal with loss at some point in their lifetime. The loss of my mom and my brother early in my life has been extremely difficult. In 2011, I lost my dad to lung cancer and was with him til the end. Since then I had been trying to figure out how to deal with death due to it being so much a part of my life. The year that followed my dad's death was depressing, complicated, and dark. Receiving two treasures, my dad's dog tags, and my grandmother's chandelier, meant so much to me, my attitude, and my outlook on my own life. With these keepsakes, I felt their presence and their love all around me. I knew that others in my situation had to feel the same way. If so, I wanted to help. So that became my mission....to help others talk about their loved ones who have passed and to tell their stories of their own personal keepsakes. Our military is very precious to me. We owe so much to our veterans that have served and protected our country. So that became my theme of my second book, Dedications: Dads & Daughters, daughters telling stories of their dads' service to our country.

People were so excited, emotional, happy, and sad all in one, but it was all good. We laughed and cried talking about memories and stories of loved ones. Sometimes, those feelings are buried deep down due to the crazy hectic lives we all live, and sometimes it just hurts too much to think or talk about. Everyone's comments were so supportive and positive. It really became a healing to all and made people feel good.

So, in this hectic life, I decided to create a series of books titled "Unforgettable Faces and Stories". We all need to stop and think about people in our lives, both past and present, and stories of those unforgettable magic moments. Those moments consists of happy memories whether with our pets, traveling the roads, or particular topics of life.......our theme is...YOUR story told by YOU! We provide a creative outlet to enable people to tell their own story, share their own pictures of special moments in their lives, and hopefully to use this storytelling as a healing process as it was for me. The third book in the Unforgettable Faces & Stories series, Best Friends: Forever and Ever published in November 2013 is comprised of heartwarming stories of friendship that everyone can relate to. Our books also present a way to give back to the community with a percentage of profit of each book going to a specific charity related to that book's theme. The fourth book in our series, Pet Tales: Unconditional Love was published in July 2014. No matter what type of animal, pets provide many of us with companionship, unconditional love, security, healing and in some cases they are trained to assist us to enable our lives to be more functional. This book is filled with stories of these very special relationships. And now we are pleased to add Letters To Heaven to the Unforgettable Faces & Stories series!

TESTIMONIALS

"I was thrilled to read another book written by Eileen Doyon called Pet Tales, I am a serious cat and animal lover, there are so many wonderful tales about all kinds of pets and their owners and what their animals mean to them, Can't wait till the next one comes out, great job, thanks for also letting me add my story, my cat Meckie from East Berlin her books will make a lot of people happy, great job, Eileen Doyon, can't wait to see you in New Hampshire." – Ulla Marggraf on Amazon.com 8/4/2014

Heart warming and inspiring. What an incredible read and sharing of Pet Tales by Eileen Doyon. Heart warming stories of people's pets and inspiring stories from service animals such as The Mighty Quinn. Randy Pierce, from 2020 Vision Quest, shared an amazing story of the work between he and Quinn. Tears came to my eyes as I read their inspiring and up lifting story. I was truly amazed while reading at their accomplishments. I look forward to seeing Randy in person and his speaking engagements to hear more of his work. Thank you Eileen Doyon for sharing these stories!" -Kathleen Roderick on Amazon.com 8/5/14

I am enjoying the stories very much and am so honored to be a part of the book. I love the cover and smile every time I see my precious Buffy sitting there. Thank you so very much for including us in the book, using our photos, and putting Buffy on the cover. Your thoughtfulness has touched me deeply." –Brenda

I didn't think the previous books in the Unforgettable Faces and Stories series by Eileen Doyon could be topped, but I think it's been done! I absolutely love Pet Tales!!! The stories are fun and sad, entertaining and written from the hearts of the owners……..and a couple are even written from the perspective of the pet! Very creative. I only wish now that I had written a story myself, but I'm guessing from the success of this one, I will get another chance! Great job and keep bringing us these personal stories!
- Sandy Fisher 9/13/14

"Goodness of the heart are written throughout this book; it is a keeper for your home library. Eileen is an inspiration to so many people where she welcomes all to share their stories." – posted by Kathy on Amazon.com 1/31/14

"I was honored to be a part of Unforgettable Faces & Stories: Dedications: Dads and Daughters (Daughters Remembering Their Dads Who Served in the Military) by writing a tribute to my Dad. Each story will touch your heart and make you proud of these great men who served in the military. They gave so much and asked for so little. You don't have to know the men to appreciate their stories. You will know them after you read their daughters loving tributes!" - posted by Joan Ells on Amazon.com

"This book was so good. My mother was not a sentimental person and gave away items instead of keeping them. I do not have much as a Keepsake from my mother or my father......just wonderful memories and they will never fade. Eileen has a knack for reaching out and touching the heart of others by sharing others' stories. Keep up the good work.....and I am anxiously awaiting her next book. Thank you Eileen!" - Donna Beason posted on Amazon.com

This book was amazing! Once I started reading the book I could not put it down. The stories are heartwarming. Some will make you laugh and others will make you cry but it truly is a book any pet lover would thoroughly enjoy! Eileen you are a caring and thoughtful person with such a huge heart-the fact that some of the proceeds of this book goes to a charity says it all. Thank you for letting us share our stories about our amazing pets! I can't wait to read your other books! -Donna Sears

YOUR story told by YOU! Have a story you'd like to share? Submit your photos and stories for inclusion in these future "Unforgettable Faces and Stories:"

When I Grow Up

A simple question asked to people of all ages....whether you are three or sixty three years young. What do YOU want to be when you grow up and why? What steps are you taking to get there? We would love for you to share YOUR story with us......coming soon.

The Second My Life Changed Forever

The phone rang, my baby was born, he died, my eyes saw, I did not see, I heard, I read, I forgot, I sent..... These are all things that can change your life in a second. What happened in your life that changed your life forever? We want YOU to share YOUR story and tell us about your life then as it happened, and where you are now.

Traditions

Traditions....we all have them....whether it's having pasta at every holiday, wearing the same shirt and hat during a sports game every week, planting jelly beans at Easter and then watch them magically turn the next morning into huge lollipops, the exchange of a fruit cake with family every Christmas for the past 15 years! Yes, we all have them. We want YOU to share YOUR Tradition with us. Tell us how and when it got started and how you carry them out year after year. Or perhaps you want to start a Tradition this year and why!

Motorcycle Memories

Riding season in New England is here again. Share your photos and stories of your adventures on your motorcycle. Where are your favorite rides? Who do you like to ride with? How many miles have you logged so far this season? Ride safe and have fun.

For more information on how you can contribute a story, visit our Coming Soon page at www.unforgettablefacesandstories.com/books/coming-soon

19987545R00097

Made in the USA
Middletown, DE
10 May 2015